DET. EDWIN FOWLE INVESTIGATES

Det. Edwin Fowle Investigates

John Brookland

BB
BitzaBooks

A CIP catalogue record for this book is available from the British Library.

Cover Design Bitza Books.

ISBN:978-1068645082
Published by Bitzabooks.co.uk
First Printing, 2025

To Debs my soulmate with thanks for your
patience and your editing and proof-reading skills.

Contents

1

PROLOGUE

Det. Insp. Edwin Fowle talking to Supt. Albert Taylor at the scene of the Caroline Luard murder 1908.

Alamy photo.

This book chronicles the exploits of an esteemed, much decorated and long-forgotten detective named Edwin Fowle of the Kent County Constabulary. He had a long and illustrious career in the Kent force completing an exemplary and extraordinary 42 years of loyal service from a constable with the badge number 287 in October 1890, to superintendent in charge of his own division in 1911, and retirement in 1932 collecting many accolades along the way including a police merit star and over twenty commendations.

In 1896 he was a founding member of Kent Police's detective department at their Wrens Court, Maidstone Headquarters becoming one of their first detective constables. In 1900 he was promoted to First Class Detective Sergeant and department head and in 1906 become the first Detective Inspector in the history of the force.

His time as a detective spanned exactly the Edwardian era and his beat was the entire County of Kent investigating a wide range of crimes including murder, infanticide, child rape, robbery, burglary, fraud, pick-pocketing, vagrancy, alcoholism and drug addiction.

The creation of the detective was a relatively new concept and he was among the pioneers of this new class of police officer who were soon embraced by reporters and journalists fascinated by their work and methods. Reporters admired them and would form alliances and friendships to obtain scoops on stories often turning them into celebrities particularly after detective fiction stories became popular in the 1880's and the creation of Sherlock Holmes. Edwin tended to shun them, rarely if ever giving interviews, and looked upon them as a nuisance. Nevertheless, he made quite a name for himself becoming one of the most recognised officers across the county regularly appearing in the newspapers due to the many headline cases he investigated.

Most of the thousands of crimes he investigated are lost to history, but there are scores of well documented ones, nine of which make up this compilation and have been selected to give a window into the hardships, social taboos, class divides and lack of women's rights of the time.

His total career spanned the reigns of four monarchs, during which time he experienced the emergence of motor vehicles, extensive train lines, telephones, radio communication, major advances in forensic science and innovations in policing methods as well as social transformations and changes in criminal behaviour. He seems to have taken all this in his stride managing to adapt to all the new challenges.

A policeman's lot in the late Victorian and Edwardian period was not an easy one: low pay, arduous long hours, little or no time off and no formal training. They did not have their own transport but were reliant for distance transport on horseback, train or hired cab with only the superintendents given dog carts and later horse and traps. Most police stations did not have telephones, there was no way of communicating quickly between different stations and messages were passed by telegram, post or using a runner.

Edwin and his colleagues were hampered by a lack of technological and forensic assets that modern policing enjoy. The new detectives were on a learning curve in detection methods. Finger printing was only just being trialled, CCTV and DNA testing was nearly a century in the future. There were no murder scene procedures such as approaching a murder scene "using the path of least common approach" or "bagging evidence" in order to preserve a scene of crime. Photography and record keeping was still basic. Therefore, most convictions were gained by collecting circumstantial evidence and witness testimony. The legal process was also convoluted and so solving serious crime was difficult, but despite these handicaps they remarkably managed to keep law and disorder under control.

So join Detective Edwin Fowle as he traipses the length and breadth of the County of Kent fighting crime and tackling criminals.

2

Pickpocketing, Welshing & The Terror (1910)

Detective Inspector Edwin Fowle, head of the Kent County Constabulary detective department was standing at the gates of the Dartford tramcar depot in Burnham Road with Detective Constable Apps carefully watching the throngs of people wrapped up against the cold of a January afternoon entering the yard. He was stamping his feet with his hands deep in the pockets of his long overcoat in a bid to keep warm. He was on the hunt for pick-pocket gangs, his favourite pastime. Since the increase in train lines, London gangs had used them to travel down to mingle in the crowds at the many racecourses and major events in the county and having committed their crimes then hot hotfooted it back with their ill-gotten gains. The "light-fingered fraternity," as they were familiarly referred to by the police, were a pet hate of his and always had been since he first joined the force. Dragging him out in the intense afternoon cold was another reason to dislike them. He knew they would be present; any large event attracted them particularly when the people attending contained many richer members of the community.

The two detectives examined the faces of as many of the passerby's as they could. Edwin received the odd second look from some people who probably found his face familiar as he had become one of the most recognised officers in the county, regularly featuring in the newspapers due to the many headline cases he investigated. He was not of a striking appearance being only five feet nine inches tall, but he was broad shouldered and of stout stature with a well-groomed moustache below a generous nose and projected an aura of authority. He was always smartly dressed and always wearing the fashionable derby hat and an overcoat which was proving valuable.

He was highly regarded by the public and his superiors but particularly so amongst pickpockets because of his special interest in them. One of his attributes, which he was proud of, was that he never forgot a face and he had made a point during his years as a detective to memorise the faces of pickpockets and major villains to such a point that he could recognise most members of the notorious London and Kent gangs. But it was a two-way street as they often spotted him first, but he liked to feel his presence acted as a deterrent. Despite this the criminal fraternity had a wary respect for him and gave him the honour of naming him the "pickpocket terror." Once spotted a chase and scuffle would ensue, which, when younger, he enjoyed but now mainly left to the younger officers.

They noticed their uniformed colleagues valiantly attempting to clear a path to allow a motor vehicle to drive through. Both men instinctively came to attention as they spotted the fully clad and distinctive figures of the famous politician Winston Churchill and his wife Clementine sitting in the back. Loud cheering and waving of hands and hats greeted their arrival and there was a renewed rush to follow the vehicle into the yard.

'There's the man himself,' commented Apps.

'Indeed, but we could have done without his visit. There's always trouble in an excitable crowd this size,' stated Edwin dourly.

'Well, at least I can tell the missus that I saw him which will please her.'

The air of excitement was palpable amongst those entering the gates as it was the month of the 1910 General Election and they were there to see and listen to the popular war hero Winston give a speech in support of the local Liberal candidate James Rowlands. The voting was to take place in two days' time and candidates across the country were making their last pleas to the voters. A platform had been constructed so that the thousands of attendees could get a good view. Very soon though the shed became full to capacity, and many had to stand outside the large doors in the hope of hearing the proceedings. The platform was also crowded with dozens of well-known local Liberals and celebrities and when Winston climbed up to the platform there was a loud outpouring of cheering which was renewed when Mrs Churchill also appeared. He then delivered a speech criticising the Conservatives, his former party, which was met with riotous applause and cheering.

Edwin and his colleague though were not there to listen or cheer the future Home Secretary but to prevent those intent on helping themselves to the wallets, watches and jewellery. Pickpocketing was rife and the police were fighting a losing battle in clamping down on the London gangs as well as the local thieves. He was under pressure from the Chief Constable to make more of an effort in response to adverse articles in the newspapers accusing the police of tardiness in prosecuting them; but it was easier said than done.

'I'm glad your wife will be pleased, but let's not get distracted by him. There are thieves amongst this lot, and I intend finding them.'

"But it's pointless Inspector, trying to pick them out amid this lot," responded Apps staring intently at every passing face.

'Don't you worry I'll spot them as they'll be the regulars. They just can't help themselves.'

"I think most people have arrived now.'

'Yes. It's time to mingle.'

'The problem is that they will recognise us know us, particularly you sir, so it will put them off.'

'Don't worry they'll be here somewhere.'

The two detectives began to mingle keeping a sharp look out for familiar faces or anyone acting suspiciously. Edwin was well aware of all their tricks of the trade and believed he had heard most excuses made by them when arrested but now again he came across a more original one that amused him. Just the other day when detaining a pickpocket on a freezing cold day, the villain pleaded that his right hand was so numb with cold that he didn't realise he had put it in someone else's pocket to keep warm.

Notwithstanding his distaste of their profession he was fascinated and amused by their way of life and some of their bizarre superstitions and traits. Traditionally they rarely robbed a person with a squint as this was associated with bringing on a disaster while weddings and funerals were viewed as significant venues. A purse stolen at a wedding containing gold portended the best of luck for the next six months whereas a picked pocket at a funeral courted immediate disaster. A pair of boots regularly worn without being caught were eventually cut up into small squares and given away as "lucky tokens" to their friends. A purse containing foreign money foretold a good deal of future travel.

Edwin's eye was suddenly caught by a familiar face and on further observance noticed the man had three companions. He nudged Apps and nodded towards the men, 'we're on; methinks they're up to no good.'

They kept watching as the four men began to act together with three of them using distraction tactics while the other looked closely at possible full pockets or bags.

'Shall we wait until they commit a robbery.'

'No need. I know one of them well and there is a warrant out for his arrest. I have wanted to catch up with him for a long time. Fetch a couple of constables and we'll nab the lot.'

Apps went off and returned with a couple of uniformed officers and they surrounded the four men and grabbed them. The officers dragged the struggling and swearing men up to Edwin and he eyed the leader.

'You don't recognise me do you my friend?'

'Can't say I do squire.'

'Well you should do; we have met before.'

'Have we?' the man answered derisively. 'I've only ever been in Kent once before and don't recollect you, but I meet a lot of people in my business,' he responded winking to his mates who laughed in the background.

'Sure about that?' asked Edwin again.

'Yeh. What's all this about guvnor. We've done nothin' wrong.'

'Did you hear of four men attacking two detectives a while back and one of them being knocked to the floor and kicked.'

'Yeh I think I heard something about it. Good on them I'd say,' he sniggered causing more laughter from his friends.

'Well that detective was me and I never forget a face particularly someone who kicks me. You're under arrest.'

The smiles of the four men soon disappeared from their faces and they were led away.

*

Another crime which plagued Edwin and took up much of his time were the "welshers" at race meetings and other sporting events. Pickpockets also liked to work these same events which made it a double headache. Betting at race meetings whether local free entry events or the major tracks was perfectly legal and there were licensed bookmakers, but this didn't stop unlicensed and devious bookmakers from taking their chances.

The worst were welshers who were prolific during the Edwardian period. Their most common method or "dodge" was to gather all the bets and then abscond with the money. Like pickpockets most welshers hailed from London and travelled down by train and made their way on foot or lifts to the race meet. There were usually two involved, the actual bookmaker who stood on a box, took the bets, shouted the odds, and handed out the betting slips. By his side was a so-called clerk who kept the "bag" containing the money, and sometimes another hired man who acted as a "crow." Crows were paid by the crooked bookies to stand in a prominent position where they could see which horses were winning at the last bend entering the straight and if the favourite was winning would signal the bookmaker who would "clear" by collecting up the gear with the clerk and "scarper" before any punters reached them to collect their winnings. It was quite an art in timing.

This of course upset the legitimate bookmakers and scuffles could break out and for gullible punters making a bet could be fraught with risk if they chose wrong. Edwin was under severe pressure to deal with them more toughly as the press were on their case as well. The *John Bull* newspaper in their Racing Notes column declared in June 1908: "There has been a general complaint from those attending racecourses regarding the great prevalence of welshers." *The Herne Bay Press* harried the police believing they should do far more to suppress welshers and suggested they ban "wrong 'uns" who were well known to them. The paper accused them of using the wrong tactics trying to catch them in the act, which often resulted with the innocent punters unfairly losing their money, rather than preventing the crime from happening. The newspaper felt police "should display a little more energy in protecting the public from welshers on both the free and other courses. Better to prevent or deter them which would also stop wasting court time." The judiciary got involved when Lord Chief Justice Cockburn promised that he would imprison welshers caught in the act and suggested customers should get redress by having a share of any money found on the bookmaker. Race organisers were also getting frustrated and the *Maidstone and Kentish Journal* reported on an ingenious deterrent that the organisers of the Mid Kent Hunt races had come up with for welshers:

> On Saturday we were much struck at the excellent arrangements made by the stewards for the convenience of welshers at the meeting in Sutton Valence There is a pond in the field near where the bookmakers set up their stands and in the middle of this pond a stake had been driven in with a sign attached stating "Specially arranged for welshers to be thrown in."

Welshers had to run the gauntlet of angry punters because amazingly they often returned to the same racecourse taking bets in a different ring where they hoped it was unlikely the same punters would be but were often recognised and attacked or arrested by the police. When arrested the more ingenious ones would claim to be "cleaned out" and show their empty pockets but pacify their punters by offering to take their names and addresses with the promise of paying them the next day. If this didn't work they would pay a small percentage of the winnings and promise the rest. A vast number of swindling bookmakers would after a good week return to London and blow all their winnings on "riotous living" and have no money left to meet their losses.

*

George Alfred Pearce was a well-known welsher who lived in 26 Bolingbroke Road in Shepherds Bush London and travelled all round the country attending meetings but liked Kent due to its proximity and ease of reach by train. He was a wily underhand operator and operated under the name of Jack Gould and always had a clerk with him.

On Tuesday 4 April 1907 he was attending the West Kent Point to Point meeting at the village of Leigh near Tonbridge. He had walked to the meet with his clerk who carried his tote board and easel while he carried the box. On arrival he always made sure to set up his box and board between two well-known regular local bookmakers beyond reproach to make himself appear respectable and trustworthy. He placed his bag containing the betting slips at his side.

He was a confident fellow and knew that he was quite adept at swindling his customers and escaping unnoticed. He could often pick out any police who were keeping the bookmakers under their watchful eyes, but it was worth the risk as they could not be at every meeting.

On this particular day he had not spotted Edwin and Detective Constable Everett patrolling the arena where the bookmakers were lined up. Edwin knew if there was to be any trouble at these events it normally broke out near them. Also visiting the meeting that day was Reuben Ovenden, a commercial traveller. He wandered the line of bookies standing on their small podiums and came across George who was displaying good odds, so he decided to place a bet with him. George gave him four to one on a horse named Starlight in the second race which was a popular horse that day. The word on the track was that he was odds on favourite to win, but this didn't stop him accepting Reuben's bet which he paid in half sovereigns. He was not the only "Jack Gould" punter on the same horse: William Hunt, another commercial traveller, had also placed a fifteen shilling to five-shilling bet on the favourite Starlight.

Reuben wandered back track-side and was excited to see Starlight get a good start and to be up with the leaders. As the horses reached the winning straight he began enthusiastically cheering the horse on and to Reuben's great excitement it won easily. Meanwhile George got the signal from his crow that the horses were on the final bend and that the favourite was winning so he climbed off his box told his compatriot to scarper with the board, picked up his bag and hurried behind the stand. He lifted out a brown mackintosh and changed his hat to disguise his appearance then eased himself through the crowd of spectators.

Reuben was ecstatic at his win and hurried to the line of bookmakers. He walked along the line but could not spot George Pearce alias Jack Gould. Also walking up and down and crossing Reuben was a concerned William who was also discovering that Jack Gould had mysteriously disappeared. Fortunately for them Edwin and Everett had spotted George hurrying away before the race had finished which was a sure sign to them that he was about to welsh on his customers. They lost sight of him behind the stand but then when he reappeared wearing a different coat and hat the two officers knew what was occurring so headed towards the fast-disappearing figure.

One of the advantages of rank and senior age was that he could leave the chasing down of suspects to younger and fitter subordinates, so he shouted to Everett. "George Pearce is on his toes, get after him. You're younger than me. And quicker."

Edwin pointed in the direction of the running man who had quite a start. He watched with a smile, egging on Everett as he chased through the crowd many of which watched with interest. George extricated himself from the crowd and ran into an adjacent field with the detective hot on his heels. Edwin followed at what he liked to describe as a fast amble. George ran along the hedgerow trying to keep out of sight, but he was encumbered by the box and bag and was none too fit. Everett soon caught up with him and grabbed hold of him. He made no attempt to put up fight.

Everett said, 'What's your game, then. Running away like that?'

'I thought you were after my money. What's your problem?'

'I am a police officer and am arresting you on suspicion of welshing.'

'How was I to know you were a bobby if you dress in those clothes.'

'You know what's up. Don't give me that old rubbish.'

Edwin reached the gate to the field and could see two other possible welshers running away in the opposite direction who having seen the commotion decided to leg it as well. Edwin knew it was pointless trying to catch them but knew other punters would have been fleeced by them. In fact more than a dozen other men also lost their winnings that day. When Everett reached Edwin with the prisoner he asked, 'When are you ever going to learn?'

'Don't know what you are talking abowt.'

'It's court again for you George.'

'Is that really necessary. Won't you give me a chance to pay up and we'll call it sorted.'

'No chance. I'd have you all locked up for good if I could for the trouble you cause me.'

Edwin told Everett to escort George to the stewards' marquee where Edwin was approached by Reuben and William who reported that they had been welshed on and he told them to accompany him into the marquee where Everrett was standing over a disconsolate George sitting in a chair.

'Is this the man who you made bets with earlier?' Edwin asked the two men.

'It is and he needs locking up. I want my money back,' Reuben shouted at him.

'Calm down, sir. Do you mind waiting outside while we interview him. The detective will come out and take a statement from both of you in a minute.'

'I'm going to search you. Clever idea the coat by the way but not a very good attempt at disguising yourself.' Edwin informed George. He checked all his pockets and emptied his bag but only found thirteen shillings and sixpence on him.

'Where's the rest of it?' Edwin asked.

'Rest of what?'

'You know what.'

'Honest that's all I took today.'

'Don't give me that. I saw you slip some money to your pal just before you scooted.'

'What pal. I was paying out some winnings.'

'I don't think so. The man was your clerk.'

'Clerk? You're having a laugh. Anyway, how did I know that the horse had won?'

'You knew a mile off as the crows would have told you.'

'If you had me under observation why did you not arrest me at the time?'

'You know I can't arrest you until the race is won and you are a quarter of a mile away.'

'News to me, officer.'

'You're a London bookie aren't you. Why not stay there. We don't want you down here. According to the stewards this is the second time you've attempted to make a book here.'

'You must know officer. Thanks to those damn Quakers you can't make a decent penny anymore on the streets, so I have to work the meetings.'

In the early 1900s Seebohm Rowntree of chocolate fame and movements like the Quakers, had formed the National Anti-Gambling League to stop the working classes from gambling. Under their pressure the Government had introduced the Street Betting Act 1906 which made it illegal for street and any off-racecourse ready money betting. George had been a starting price bookie on the streets of London prior to the Act and had been prosecuted for street betting and fined five pounds so had decided to change tack and try his luck at on course betting. When he went to court the magistrates were not as lenient this time and gave him six week's imprisonment.

*

Edwin and D.C. Apps were on duty at the Tickham Hunt races near Milsted just south of Sittingbourne on the 3 April 1908. They had arrived early keeping an eye on the bookies who were setting up their stalls. They were once again on the lookout for welshers. It had been a quiet morning so far, but the first race didn't begin until 12.30pm. The first two races passed without any incident along bookies row then after the third race they could see a commotion occurring in the crowd and Edwin sent Apps to check out what was causing it. A large vociferous and jostling crowd was gathering around one of the bookies and Apps had to really struggle to push his way through the throng to where the altercation was taking place. Although he kept shouting 'make way there for the police' everyone was more intent on the uproar and either ignored or didn't hear him.

Eventually he made it to a stand where several men were shouting 'pay up or you're going to get it' and other aggressively threatening suggestions of violence. The men were egged on by the excited crowd. Apps bravely stood between the men and the cowering bookie, and he shouted to the mob that he was a police officer and ordered them to calm down. 'What's wrong here.'

'Plenty,' shouted back one of the aggressive men.

'He's welshing on our bets,' shouted another.

The bookie kept shouting back, 'I'm all cleaned out mate.'

'You've got my money for a start,' shouted one angry man.

'And my money,' said another.

'I tell ya. I've got no money. I can't pay out at the moment.'

The upset punters then closed in on the bookie again and things began to get out of control. Edwin had seen that a serious disturbance was brewing, and that Apps was outnumbered and in trouble, so he was pushing his way towards him to give support. On arrival he and Apps stood in front of the bookie to protect him as the crowd were intent on mobbing him. Edwin tried to calm the situation and told them to stand aside, or he would call constables to move them. Eventually they unwillingly parted, and the two officers escorted the bookie holding tightly to his arms. As they walked down the avenue of people Edwin shouted, 'We are taking him to the luncheon tent. Anyone who thinks they have been robbed by this man can follow us. The rest of you get back to the races and disperse.'

'Ere, who are calling a robber,' uttered the bookie.

'Shut up,' replied Apps sternly.

They headed for the luncheon tent followed by a small group of enraged punters. The tent was relatively empty as lunch was over, but a few people were sipping tea and eating cake and were surprised and somewhat startled by Edwin's appearance with the handcuffed prisoner and an entourage of angry men. Edwin then tried to get to the bottom of what had happened to enrage everyone. He called in one of the men who wanted the bookie arrested for welshing on his bet.

His name was Thomas Reeves, a local Faversham man, who had backed a horse with him in the second race which came second but in the third race he handed over a pound for a two pounds ten shillings return on a horse named Tuppence to win and the bookmaker handed him a betting ticket with a name of Slater stamped on it. The horse duly won. On returning to the bookie's row he could not find the man purporting to be the bookie. There were other men searching for him. On looking around he spotted the man in the crowd and shouted to the others, 'there he is. That's Slater.'

They rushed over to him and demanded their money. He told them, 'I'm not Slater. That's not my name. An argument ensued and that's when you intervened.' he told Edwin.

He turned to the bookie and demanded, 'What's your name.'

'Nathen Saffer, guv'nor.'

'And where are you from Mr Saffer?'

'I'm down from London. Live in Stratford. Leytonstone Road to be exact. An East End fella.'

'What is your story. Are you a bookie?'

'Not really sir. I work for a Mr Lee Davis.'

'Doing what?'

'I'm his clerk.'

Edwin turned to Apps, 'See if you can find this Mr Davis and whether he employs this guy.'

'So why do people think your name is Slater and why are all these people so upset with you?' he asked Saffer.

'I've no idea,' he innocently replied.

'You'll have to do better than that.'

It's a bit of a long story Guv'nor.'

'Tell me.'

'Well I came down on the 9.18am train from London Bridge station to meet up with Mr Davis as I am his clerk. I forgot to change trains at Strood so got delayed and didn't get to Maidstone until about eleven. I then messed about a bit in town and then went to Milsted arriving at the racecourse about 2pm. I couldn't find my boss at first but when I did he said I was late and there was nothing for me to do.'

'Is there an end to this tale?' interrupted Edwin.

'Well. With nothing to do I went and stood by Joe Barnett, the local bookmaker, and watched him. Then there was a kerfuffle next to him and a crowd started tearing up his stuff saying he was a welsher, so I helped him.'

'Is that right,' said Edwin sarcastically.

'Well guv'nor, if I was a welsher do you think I would have stayed there and waited for them to get me?'

At this point Apps returned and informed Edwin that Saffer was indeed this Davis bookmaker's clerk.

'I don't believe a word of it,' said Edwin, 'I think that because you were losing out with no work for your boss you decided to make some money on the side.'

'Not at all sir.'

'I'm arresting you on suspicion of welshing.' Edwin then cautioned him.

'You can't do that. I've told you what happened.'

'I can do it, and I have done it. You can give this cock and bull story to the magistrates and see if they believe you.'

Nathan Saffer appeared before the magistrates at Sittingbourne petty sessions charged with having stolen by means of a trick, known as welshing, £1 belonging to Thomas Reeves on Friday 3 April. The magistrates, like Edwin, did not believe his elaborate story that he was an innocent bystander caught up in the affray. There was in fact loud laughter from everyone in the court as he told the story. He was sentenced to pay a £2 fine or fourteen days hard labour. He paid the fine.

*

Henry James Leat was a notorious bully and thief and well known to the Metropolitan Police who knew him to be a dangerous man. He resided at 12 Maygood Street in Barnsbury, North London, not the most salubrious part of the city. They had arrested and prosecuted him before for larceny and assault and he had spent six months in prison. In November 1900 he was at the Folkestone Races in Kent and running a book in the half-crown ring under the name of Jim Merry Brighton. Also in the half-crown ring was Edwin Fowle keeping an eye on things.

A local jeweller named Josephus Edwards was enjoying his afternoon at the races and placed a bet with Henry Leat by putting five shillings on a horse named Rambling Katie in the third race. In return Henry gave him what looked like a legitimate ticket with the name Merry stamped on it and the number fourteen printed in red. Josephus returned to track-side and watched as Rambling Katie duly won the race. He excitedly went to claim his winnings handing Henry the ticket who stood to his full height and towered over Josephus while he surveyed it and then laughed.

'You've got the wrong ticket, matey,' he said.

'What do you mean. It's the ticket you gave me.'

'Afraid not Guv. The ticket should have the number twenty-two on it, not fourteen.'

'But this is the ticket you gave me. It's your mistake not mine.'

'I'd be careful if I was you friend. Are you suggesting that I'm a thief or something?' he said threateningly.

'Well no, but the horse won, and this is the slip you gave me.'

'Sorry but I'm not paying out on that. Someone must have stolen the ticket from you.'

'But that's absurd. I've had it in my hand the whole time.'

'Listen mate, if you know what's good for you you'd better shove off.'

'I shall do no such thing. Give me my winnings.'

Henry then used what was described as very bad language. Edwin who was standing ten yards away suddenly heard the raised voices and swearing and immediately made his way over to the bookie and the irate man standing next to him. There was some scuffling taking place, so Edwin guessed what was going on, yet another welsher. A crowd had already gathered round the clash.

'What's going on here,' shouted Edwin.

'None of your business mate.'

'I think it may be my business as I'm a police officer.'

'Thank goodness,' exclaimed the relieved Josephus, 'he won't pay me my winnings, officer.'

'Is that so,' said Edwin looking at Henry.'

'Just a slight misunderstanding guv'nor. This gentleman appears to have lost his ticket.'

'I have done no such thing,' interjected Josephus, 'he is trying to swindle me.'

Josephus explained about the number on his ticket and Edwin began smiling.

'It is nothing to laugh about officer.'

'Sorry sir, but our friend here is playing an age-old trick on you.' Edwin turned to Henry, 'What is your name?'

'Henry.'

'Henry what?'

'Leat.'

'So who is this Merry?'

'That's my bookie name that I operate under.'

'Really. Well Mr Leat, or Merry, or whatever your name is I'm arresting you on suspicion of stealing five shillings from this gentleman.'

'Ere you can't do that. I'm just trying to earn an honest living.'

'As I said it is on suspicion and you will have to come to the police station while we investigate further. Now behave yourself while I search you.' Edwin ordered.

Edwin went through Henry's jacket pockets and discovered two pounds two shillings in silver, one shilling two and a half pence in bronze. In his satchel he found a large quantity of betting tickets with the name Jim Merry of Brighton. Edwin held them up to him.

'Did he make any other bets with you?'

'Well, no.'

'Then how did he get his ticket?'

'Ok, Ok I admit making a bet with the man of twenty to four on Rambling Katie, but seriously someone must have stolen his ticket, that's not the one I gave him.

'I don't believe a word of it,' stated Edwin, 'so you'll have to accompany me to the police station.'

Henry appeared before the Hythe County magistrates bench and was charged with feloniously stealing five shillings by means of a trick, the money of Josephus Edwards, a jeweller. At the hearing Henry persevered with his defence that Josephus had been robbed of his ticket and another one substituted for it but claimed he had paid out the winnings to another man who presented the number fourteen ticket. The magistrates didn't fall for his excuses and sentenced him to a month's hard labour in prison. Henry then tried some emotional blackmail as a last resort by asking 'can't you make it a fine as I have a poor widowed mother to look after,' to which the magistrates gave a definite no. Josephus asked for his five shillings to be returned which was granted and it was taken out of the money found on Henry.

3

A Body in the Village Pond (1906)

Infanticide was the most traumatic crime the police investigated in the period.

British Newspaper Archive

The most tragic, traumatic and emotional crime that Edwin and his colleagues had to deal with was infanticide, the killing of newborn babies, also known as infant homicide. Investigating these was profoundly disturbing for him being a deeply religious man, but he was also a compassionate person which often revealed itself during his inquiries. Infanticide was sadly a common occurrence in the Edwardian period as it had been throughout Victorian times and for that matter right through human history. It was so commonplace that Mrs Baines in her 1866 *Journal of Social Sciences* wrote: "It has been said that the police, with too much truth, think no more of finding the body of a dead child in the streets than of picking up a dead dog or cat."

So common was it in the period that in 1862 Dr William Burke Ryan wrote in his book *Infanticide : its law, prevalence, prevention and history*:

> The feeble wail of murdered childhood in its agony assails our ears at every turn and is borne on every breeze. The sight is horrified as, day after day, the melancholy catalogue of murders meets the view, and we try to turn away the gaze in hope of some momentary relief. But turn where we may, still we are met by the evidence of a widespread crime. In the quiet of the bedroom we raise the box-lid, and the skeletons are there. In the calm evening walk we see in the distance the suspicious-looking bundle, and the mangled infant within. By the canal side, or in the water, we find the dead child. In solitude of the wood we are horrified by the ghastly sight; and if we betake ourselves to the rapid rail in order to escape the pollution, we find a journey's end that the mouldering remains of a murdered innocent have been

our travelling companion; and that the odour from that unsuspected parcel truly indicates what may be found within.

Having a baby out of wedlock was still taboo and the fear of being socially ostracised and unable to work affected most women's decisions after they gave birth, particularly if they were unable to return home or left the workhouse with nowhere to go. Those single mothers who managed to find jobs had the difficult problem of finding child care, often with unsuitable women.

The term infanticide was originally a medical term used to describe alleged temporary insanity caused to women by the trauma of giving birth, a view that was widely accepted by doctors, and a condition that was known as Puerperal insanity or Puerperal mania. Doctors believed this illness lasted for six weeks after birth and defence solicitors began using this excuse in court to exonerate mothers. Infanticide was viewed as a lesser crime than murdering an adult. The reasons for killing their new born were based mainly on social, economic and religious influences although some desperate women viewed it purely as an act of delayed abortion.

What made it so traumatic for the police was the methods used to kill the babies. The most common being strangulation, suffocation and drowning. The bodies were normally dumped in public spaces like parks, streets, ponds and hedgerows often in plain sight.

Many young women from rural areas like Kent, migrated to the cities especially London to find jobs in domestic service and fell prey to their employers, male colleagues or boyfriends who gave false promises of marriage but on becoming pregnant were jilted only to be thrown out of work by their masters and mistresses. Half of all illegitimate children born in the period were conceived by women in service.

When nearly full-term women with nowhere to go entered workhouse infirmaries to have their child or lying-in hospitals funded by charities. Soon after birth they were referred to their local parish who under the law were duty bound to look after them financially. Workhouses and local authorities did often try and trace the fathers and hold them to account and on occasions forced marriages of pregnant single women to a man who was viewed as a friend or believed to be the father, known as 'knob-stick weddings' were arranged, but most resulted in the husband abandoning the mother.

Unfortunately for many, their only recourse was to rid themselves of their babies by murdering them at birth. The death penalty was still on the Statute book for infanticide and although no women were actually executed in Britain after 1847 many mothers still had this threat literally hanging over them.

*

Norman Dolley, a farm worker, lived in a typical labourers abode named Chapel Cottage in the village of Knockholt five miles north west of the town of Sevenoaks. At about 2pm on Thursday afternoon 20 December 1906 he was walking back to work through Randall's Wood at Randall's Corner in Knockholt, a quiet little frequented spot. He came out of the wood along a path into a field with a pond situated in the corner five yards from the field boundary and from there a track led from Pratts Bottom to Knockholt. He could see something floating on the surface on the far side which he believed might be a dead animal. He walked round the periphery keeping his eye on the item which wasn't moving. As he got closer it looked like a package of some sort and intrigued, he stood on the bank and crouched with hands on his knees to get a closer look.

To his horror he saw a tiny arm and a leg just visible beneath the surface of the water but then realised it must be a discarded or lost child's doll perhaps after a picnic, although it was an isolated spot that few people visited. He broke off a stick from the hedge and used it to pull the doll through the foot deep water which was choked with leaves and mud. It was at this point that he realised it was the body of a baby. At first he staggered back feeling sick but steeled himself and pulled the baby's body onto the bank. The poor child was clothed in a flannel binder and a white shirt with blue stripes. To add to the revulsion he noticed a piece of rag protruding from the baby's mouth. He was in a state of shock and paced up and down in a dither not sure what to do next; take the body somewhere or leave it there to go for help. He decided to rush off and try and find the village constable but bumped into another villager and told him to contact the police while he returned to keep watch.

Sergeant Strood of Knockholt police received the news of the discovery at 2.30pm and made his way to the scene as quickly as he could, finding Norman in an agitated state. Norman quickly informed him that he had removed the body from the pond. The sergeant having children of his own knelt down and examined the tiny bundle and soon ascertained it was a girl and very young perhaps only a month old. He noted a white handkerchief protruding about two inches out of the mouth. He then searched the bank of the pond for footprints and any other clothing but could find none.

'How long has it been in there do you reckon?' asked Norman.

'I'm no expert but I should say at least a week.'

'The water level was much higher a couple of weeks ago after all that rain we 'ad when it was flooded,' stated Norman.

'You're right there. The body probably wasn't visible until the level dropped.'

'What are you going to do with the poor mite?'

'Too late to get it to the mortuary at Sevenoaks. I'll have to take the body to Knockholt police station and keep it overnight.'

'Rather you than me.'

'I'll see you tomorrow for a statement.'

'Righto,' said Norman walking off down the track muttering expletives to himself and leaving the sergeant to it.

When Strood arrived at the police station a message was immediately sent to the divisional headquarters in Sevenoaks where the superintendent in charge, Albert Taylor, was informed on the tragedy. Albert was a well-known figure in the area being a rather flamboyant character. He was fifty years old with handsome features hidden under an exaggerated handlebar moustache and beard and stood over six feet tall with a military bearing. He set about making discreet inquiries which pointed towards a certain local young woman. He then followed protocol by contacting the detective department in Maidstone which investigated and made-up cases for serious crime on his behalf.

*

Bertha Mary Stone was born in 1887 to parents John and Mary Stone at 5 Hope Cottage, Longford, Dunton Green, a small hamlet just a few miles southeast of Knockholt. It was a thriving, mainly agricultural community well known for its large water driven corn mill. It was a poor household, just a workers cottage and she received little education. At a young age she was forced to look for work to help supplement the household income and like most young girls of the time from rural areas, the only real avenue for work was as a household servant. If they were lucky they might get a position at a large country estate near home but these were very rare so many tended to gravitate to nearby large towns or to London to find work where such jobs were infinite. Unfortunately most of these country girls were rather naïve of city life and were easily manipulated and preyed upon often becoming pregnant with little hope of marriage. This unhappily was to be Bertha's future.

In 1905, aged eighteen, she found a position as a servant in a London house. She was a good-looking girl and often told she looked older than her age and soon found admirers. She had been happily working for just over a year when in April 1906 the unwanted telltale symptoms of pregnancy began to panic her. She was well aware of what this would mean. Unmarried pregnant women were considered morally fallen and faced intense social stigma. Raising a child out of wedlock was incompatible with maintaining respectability and employment. She had few options; she could consider giving the baby to a foundling hospital, risk an extremely dangerous illegal abortion, or give birth in a workhouse infirmary. She could also go back to her parents, but many small communities often ostracized unmarried mothers.

She did her best to conceal her condition from her fellow workers and her employer, a familiar story played out thousands of times in servant households nationwide. By the time she was seven months pregnant it was impossible to hide it any longer and found it difficult to work, and she recognised that her employer would probably have little sympathy and no doubt let her go. Most of her fellow servants were now well aware of her condition and told her to get herself admitted to a workhouse infirmary.

On September 20, 1906, with the birth only about six weeks away, she followed their advice and out of desperation applied to the St Pancras Workhouse Infirmary. She had heard the workhouse was reasonably safe and well organised as many were harsh, overcrowded, unsanitary and lacked adequate medical facilities. There were many horror stories of women dying while giving birth and the mortality rate of new born babies was high. It was not easy to gain acceptance and she had to plead her case at an interview with the relieving officer and workhouse master. Her details were diligently entered into a huge leather-bound ledger and the Board of Guardians at their weekly meeting finally gave the final approval, despite her circumstances not being as dire as many others. Perhaps they saw hope of her turning her life around as she had a determined character.

The workhouse and infirmary was a huge facility accommodating thousands of men, women, children and babies attended to by a legion of staff, nurses and matrons. She was admitted to the maternity wing and introduced to nurse Annie Harling who was assigned to attend her on a daily basis. During the weeks awaiting the birth, Bertha worked in the kitchens, laundry, cared for newborns on the ward and helped the mothers during labour and was regarded as a willing and industrious worker, generally liked and having "a quiet and nice character."

Bertha began her confinement on 5 November and gave birth at 4.50 pm to a 6lb 13oz baby girl; the nurses describing her as "a nice little thing." The infirmary provided uniform baby clothing consisting of a Scotch plaid flannel hat and binder, a white blue striped frock and bootees as well as flannel nappies. Most newly born were breast fed but Bertha struggled and was described by Annie as not being very "robust." Her health improved following the birth as did that of the baby who she named Freda, and she was duly registered and christened. Bertha appeared to adore her but as time went by she became more unsettled, impatiently asking to leave immediately. She told the staff that having had the baby there was no need to remain, and she wanted to go home to her parents. The matron would not hear of it as they preferred to keep new mothers at least a month to ensure that there were no complications. They would not let her go until they were satisfied arrangements had been put in place to guarantee the ongoing well-being of her and Freda.

Eventually Bertha remained at the infirmary for a further three weeks before she got her wish. It was recorded that she looked after Freda well and was devoted to her, describing her as a "very good mother." Under the Poor Law, Parish Councils in which a mother was born, were duty bound to look after them if they had no means of support. Single mothers were often passed from one place to another as parishes often couldn't or were unwilling to pick up the costs. Having not been born in London the workhouse contacted Bertha's home authorities to negotiate taking her. Eventually they begrudgingly accepted responsibility but Annie wasn't convinced that Bertha's mother had agreed to take her, so unbeknown to her, the workhouse arranged for the nurse, who had become a friend, to transfer her in a taxi to a local workhouse while this was confirmed.

She was discharged on the 24 November and after having breakfast at 8.45am Annie took her from the female quarters to the waiting taxi, saying goodbye to the many friends she had made during her two month stay. She was taken to the Ide Hill Union Workhouse in Sevenoaks, just a few miles from the village of Dunton Green, where her parents lived. She was handed over under protest to the stern labour mistress, Grace Thurtle, who placed her in the receiving ward and was to supervise her stay. Grace was in charge of dispensing all the duties that the inmates were expected to do to earn their keep.

Bertha insisted that she wanted to leave straight away but the workhouse had not received confirmation from her mother that she would welcome her and the normal procedure when moving from one workhouse to another was to give 24 hours' notice to leave. She was confused, depressed and uncertain what to do. Finally she asked for pencil and paper and wrote a letter to her mother asking if she could return home. Her mother reluctantly agreed so she immediately gave notice and next day after taking breakfast she left the workhouse on foot at 8.45am on the 26th. to head home with Freda in her arms. She was unsure of the quickest way out of Sevenoaks and asked the staff for directions to Dunton Green and began walking the four and half mile route along the quiet Back Lane that should have taken her at most two hours.

Bertha rested in a field, cradling and kissing Freda, fretting about the poor future Freda would have with her and how people would treat her. By this time, her thoughts had led to despair and disturbed her mind and thinking. So she sat and cried and fell into the depths of hopelessness. Seven hours later at 4pm, she arrived home, looking very depressed and unwell. Her mother fussed over her, but Bertha ate little and said even less. When her mother asked about Freda, she claimed a friend in London was looking after her. Days went by without mention of Freda, making her mother suspicious. A week later, pressed for answers, Bertha said Freda was fine and told her mother she was fed up with all the questioning and was going to care for a sick friend who lived in a nearby village.

*

Edwin received news of the case from Albert at 10am on the 21 December and made his way to Knockholt Police station where he met up with him and was informed of the facts known so far.

'So our main suspect is this girl, Bertha Stone?' summed up Edwin.

'That's the gossip in the village. She apparently turned up recently and was seen carrying a baby, then both her and the baby disappeared so she might be our mother.'

'Do we know much about her?'

'Well, we have done some door knocking and have several eye witness accounts that she was in the area. We have one particularly good witness, a Helen Hill who lives at Single Cross Knockholt. She knows Bertha and saw her at midday carrying a baby in a shawl going in the direction of Randall's corner. Her house is only four hundred yards from the pond.'

'Was the baby alive? asked Edwin, 'did she hear it crying.'

'Unfortunately she cannot confirm that either way, but as she says the pond is not on a route Bertha would have taken from the workhouse to Dunton Green.'

'Which means if it is her baby it means she discarded the child on a sudden impulse on her way home which seems strange. She had plenty of opportunity before. It is an awful thing to undertake.'

'Sadly, yes, but as you are aware Edwin these women are not normally in their right mind after giving birth.'

'So the doctors tell us. I think the best way forward is to go to the parent's house in Dunton Green and interview them,' stated Edwin.

'I agree,' confirmed Taylor.

'Do we know the whereabouts of this girl?'

'Not at present, but we are making enquiries.'

Edwin and Taylor went by carriage to the parent's address where they were let in by a very nervous Mary Stone. The superintendent had the difficult job of informing her that they had found the body of a baby which they believed was her granddaughter. Mary could not quite grasp the news and informed them that her daughter's baby was in London with a friend. They broke the news that they believed this was not the case. When the implications of what they were telling her finally dawned on her she had to sit down in a state of shock.

'This is a very serious inquiry, and it is imperative for the sake of your daughter as much as anything else that we ascertain the full facts.'

'I understand, sir,' Mary muttered back.

'Do you know where your daughter is?'

'Yes, she stayed with us a couple of weeks and then went to look after a sick friend over in the village of Riverhead. She's been there for the last three weeks or so.'

Edwin looked at the superintendent and nodded, 'How far is Riverhead from here?'

'Just over a mile away. Just a half hour walk,' replied the superintendent.

'When did your daughter come home?' Edwin continued.

'It was on 26 November, sir.'

'About what time. Do you remember?'

'It was about four o'clock.'

'I take it you were expecting her?'

Yes sir. She wrote and told us.'

'And you knew that before coming here she had been in London?'

'She'd had a job as a housemaid for nearly a year.'

'Were you aware that she became pregnant while in London and went into the workhouse to give birth.'

'She had written and told us.'

'But you never went up to see her?'

'No.'

Why was that?'

'It costs money we don't have.'

'Were you happy she was coming to stay with you?'

'Of course. We were looking forward to it.'

'So when she arrived without the baby were you surprised?'

'We were. I asked straight away where it was, and she said she had left it with a friend in London to look after.'

'Did you wonder why?'

'I was surprised and disappointed. I asked her but she didn't really answer.'

'How did she look when she arrived home?'

'Not well sir. She did not look up to much, pale and ill looking.'

'Was she upset or anxious?'

'Not that I noticed.'

'Did she ever mention the baby again while she was here?'

'No sir.'

'Alright. Thank you Mrs Stone. That is all for now.'

Edwin turned to the superintendent and said, 'Time to get over to Rivershead and talk to Miss Stone.'

'I believe so,' agreed the Superintendent.

They got into their carriage and went to 2 The Heights, Riverhead where Bertha was living, and having introduced themselves entered the cottage.

Edwin asked Bertha, 'We are here on a serious matter Miss Stone. We have found the dead body of a female child in a pond at Randall's corner and I have reason to suspect that you are the mother of that child. Am I correct in that belief?'

Bertha fell back into a chair with a bewildered expression and was lost for words before exclaiming miserably, 'It is my child.'

'In that case, Bertha Stone I am arresting you on suspicion of wilfully murdering your female child at Knockholt on or about the 26 November last. You are not obliged to say anything unless you wish to do so, but whatever you say may be taken down in writing and used against you.'

Edwin and Albert escorted her from the house and took her to Knockholt police station where Edwin read the charge again and she repeated that the child had been hers.

*

The inquest was held on Christmas Eve Monday 24 December at Knockholt police station before Mr H B Sewell, Coroner for West Kent. It proved to be a disorderly and entertaining affair. Henry Bond was elected foreman of the jury. Bertha was driven to the inquest accompanied by a Mrs Aldridge, a leading women's rights advocate who regularly visited female prisons to support young girls in a similar situation and had heard of her plight in the newspapers.

Norman Dolley was the first to give evidence of finding the body and Sergeant Strood told the part he had played in removing it. Annie Harling the nurse had been summoned from London to give evidence and was visibly upset having become quite attached to her. She informed the court that the baby was fully formed, had gained weight during her stay and that Bertha was in good health on leaving. She was shown Freda's clothing which again brought a tears to her eyes. She identified the shirt as being the one given to the baby at the workhouse but could not confirm the binder. Annie was very forthright at one point and said that Bertha was a nice, quiet girl, willing and a good worker and raised her voice by saying "and a good mother." There were several shouts of "Hear, Hear" at this point from certain members of the public. Annie continued by saying that she had never been called upon to speak to Bertha about the way she was treating the child. Grace Thurtle from the Sevenoaks workhouse was also called and confirmed Bertha was in good health and was in a hurry to leave and go to her parents. Bertha's mother was then interviewed by the coroner.

Doctor William Taylor was next up and repeated the findings he had given to the police. At one point he was asked by a juror if any signs of poisoning had been detected and the doctor was rather embarrassed to admit that he couldn't answer as he didn't analyse the contents of the stomach thinking it unnecessary which raised some eyebrows amongst the jurors. Edwin gave evidence from the interviews with witnesses and then it was the moment that all the assembled onlookers were waiting for, the interviewing of Bertha. Throughout the proceedings she had sat cowed and quietly sobbing into a handkerchief while Mrs Aldridge had valiantly tried to calm her. When Sewell addressed her she immediately cried out loud and went into fits of sobbing to such an extent she was incoherent and it was impossible to get her attention. Sewell asked her several times if she wanted to give evidence, but he received no reply. Eventually he declared her unfit to be interviewed.

With Bertha admitting her guilt he reluctantly had no choice but to sum up the evidence and instruct the jury that "I see no doubt that this was a case of wilful murder."

In answer to this a juror raised his hand and requested, 'is it not possible to bring in a lesser charge?'

The coroner looked at him and reluctantly replied, 'I don't think so.'

Another juryman then got involved and asked, 'Is there no more evidence to prove that it was death by suffocation?'

'We have a doctor's statement which clearly shows it was by suffocation,' said the coroner rather frustrated.

Henry Bond, the foreman then joined the conversation, 'Yes, but is there no other evidence to show that the mother actually suffocated it?'

Sewell took a deep breath, 'I don't see what other evidence is necessary. You must remember that this is not a court of law, and we are not trying her; you only have to decide the cause of death and whether there is a prima facie case to send the woman to trial. It is not your job to find her guilty or not guilty.'

Henry then begrudgingly said, 'So we have no choice but to only take the doctor's evidence in deciding the mother did it?

The coroner replied, 'That's correct but we not only have a chain of strong circumstantial evidence, but also a confession from the prisoner and the doctor has given a clear and full statement; there are other witnesses, and the police have produced a very clear case. To my mind the cause of death is clear, but you can say that death was by suffocation, and that the evidence was not sufficient to show who did it.'

It was evident from the discussions that the jurors had some empathy towards Bertha and that the mood in the room was in her favour especially as she was displaying such a pitiable sight. The jurors quickly whispered amongst themselves and much to the coroner's irritation Henry Bond would not let the matter drop and raised another point, 'We have no doubt about death being by suffocation, but we doubt whether the mother did it or somebody else.'

'Well, that's the question you must decide on,' said the exasperated coroner. 'I think it is time for you gentlemen to retire and consider your verdict in private,' he continued pleased for the chance to end the discussion.

The jury then left for their deliberations which only took about ten minutes, and once they had trooped back in, the coroner asked if they had agreed on a verdict.

Henry Bond who was obviously at this point enjoying his moment of fame replied, 'We have agreed a verdict.'

'And what is that verdict?' he prompted.

'We agree that the child had been suffocated but by whom we do not know.'

There was a loud murmuring as people digested what Henry had said and Sewell was somewhat non-plussed for a while and put his head in his hands. After a minute he looked up and said, 'so your verdict is "Wilful murder against some person or person's unknown; no evidence having been given that the mother killed the child.'

'If that's the proper way of saying it, then yes sir.'

'Well I'm pleased we have that sorted.'

His relief was short lived as suddenly one of the juryman stood and shouted, 'we are not convinced that it was the girl's child.'

Sewell was astounded by the interruption and comment and sat back in his chair shaking his head in disbelief. The court was getting quite rowdy and there was much excitement amongst the public with everyone talking to each other, many agreeing with the juror's outburst; some amused by what was occurring; some clapping and cheering. The jury was getting quite out of hand, something not often seen and it appeared they were doing everything possible to exonerate and sabotage the hearing her and perhaps influence an impending trial. The coroner attempted to convince the jury that the identity of the child had been established and explain the consequences of their actions, but they were adamant and still maintained that there was no evidence to whose child it was.

To make matters worse another juryman then objected and stated that Bertha in her hysterical state would admit to anything under these circumstances just to get it over with. Sewell was now losing control of the proceedings and getting angry and exasperated. He told the jury that if they still couldn't accept the ownership of the child he had no choice but to try and make the identification clear before they could proceed further. Henry Bond on behalf of the whole jury firmly reiterated they were not satisfied whose baby it was.

The coroner was annoyed as he now had to go through all the identification evidence again and Bertha's statement and was forced to send for the unfortunate Nurse Harling, who was still present, and inform her that she must return to the mortuary and fully identify the body again. While she was being conveyed there to repeat her unpleasant task the coroner continued in his attempt to convince the jury that the identification was correct. Unfortunately for nurse Harling, her trip proved worthless as before she returned the jury finally accepted it was Bertha's child.

To add to the coroner's woes and astonishment Superintendent Taylor and the jury insisted that the hearing records should show the body was found in the neighbouring Chelsfield Parish as the body was right on the border with Knockholt and they did not want Knockholt tarnished with the incident.

By this time there was utter confusion in the court with no one really knowing what the verdict was but eventually the coroner declared "Wilful murder against some person or person's unknown; no evidence having been given that the mother killed the child."

Probably to atone for their behaviour Henry Bond thanked Sewell on behalf of the jury members for his patience and the way he had conducted the inquest and also praised Edwin and the Superintendent for their diligence.

*

The inquest was only the beginning of the trauma that Bertha was to face as she was forced to appear in three separate magistrate's hearings over the next ten days and at each one was remanded so that the police could gather more evidence. The first hearing at the Bromley Police Court on Saturday 22 December when there was considerable excitement when Bertha appeared before the magistrates charged with feloniously, wilfully and with malice aforethought kill and slay one, Freda Stone, at Knockholt on 26 November 1906. A crowd of mainly contemptuous looking women had gathered outside the court to see her arrive and ensconced in the small courtroom which was soon filled to capacity with onlookers keen to discover her fate as most were aware that the charge could carry the death penalty.

Because the room was so crowded, and the atmosphere belligerent, Bertha had been seated in the jury box with all eyes fixed on her which made it rather flustering for the jurors. Bertha, still just nineteen years old, portrayed a pathetic sight in the box wrapped in a shawl awaiting the magistrates. Once again Mrs Aldridge was sitting next to her and unsuccessfully attempting to console her.

At half past ten two magistrates entered the court, and everyone stood. They were T C Devey Esq and G E Lewis Esq and for some reason made a point of hearing two minor cases first. This caused Bertha more agony as she sat waiting her turn and visibly lapsed into a more distraught state. Eventually she was helped into the dock and cast her eyes to the floor as she listened to Mr L Beeston, the assistant clerk read out the charge to her. She immediately burst into tears and hung her head as she realised the enormity of her predicament. As the proceedings continued the magistrates and those assembled in the court could see her distress increasing. It became obvious that the belligerent atmosphere in the room was changing and the many ladies present were beginning to show empathy towards her. She continued her sobbing and at one point looked as though she would faint so the steely magistrates who had also succumbed to her predicament stopped the proceedings and called for a drink to be brought to her. Mrs Aldridge then rushed off and returned with a glass of water.

Edwin was the first called to the stand by Mr F G Frayling, a well-known barrister representing the Treasury. He described how the case had first been reported to him and how he had gone with Superintendent Taylor first to Duncton Green and then on to number 2 The Heights, Riverhead where he interviewed the prisoner and cautioned her before taking her to Sevenoaks Police station on suspicion that she had wilfully murdered her female baby. At the station Edwin formally cautioned her, and she again admitted it was her child.

The hearing was then adjourned and she was remanded until Wednesday 3 January when Albert asked for yet another adjournment to complete more inquiries. The final magistrates hearing was held on Monday 31 December. The *Bromley Telegraph* reported that the: "courtroom was crowded with lovers of the morbid, to whose minds perhaps, the sight of a frail girl, prostrated with the weight of the most awful charge which the law enforces, represented a certain degree of piquant excitement. The spectacle which the poor girl presented during the hearing was one which could but call forth sympathy from any save the most callous heart."

Bertha was wearing a black hat and white shawl and had to be assisted into the dock as she was in a state of collapse, pale and distraught. A chair had been provided and she collapsed into it and moaned and sobbed throughout the hour's hearing. Most of the evidence was the same as that already noted at the inquest. With the evidence completed the Chairman asked Bertha, 'Do you desire to say anything?'

She quietly replied, 'No, sir.'

'Do you desire to call any witnesses at your trial?' the Chairman asked.

'No.'

'In that case I am committing you to trial at the next County Assizes. She was then helped from the court in a state of shock and resignation.

*

Her trial at the Maidstone Winter Assizes was held on Thursday February 21, 1907, in front of Mr Justice Bucknill. He was late in arriving and apologised for keeping everyone waiting until 11.50 which delayed Bertha's case. He immediately told the Grand jury it was their duty to bring in a true Bill which meant her trial could go ahead. She was indicted for "feloniously, wilfully, and of her malice aforethought killing and murdering Freda Stone, at Knockholt on the 26th. November,1906".

Police prosecutions were always difficult as juries were increasingly reluctant to commit the infanticidal mother to death and it was often difficult to prove to them that the baby had not been still born and had not taken a breath. Medical and legal professionals had difficulty in finding evidence to prove whether it had breathed independently from the mother, was strangled by the umbilical cord or deliberately suffocated.

During the Edwardian era the courts and judiciary increasingly viewed women in infanticide cases as victims of society, and they received more sympathy, and the fathers began to be villainised.

Many women's rights advocates began supporting the women in jail, court hearings and campaigned on their behalf. Prosecution was a very serious matter and being a capital offence was an automatic death penalty. As judges became more lenient viewing the act as insanity the charge was often changed to the far lesser "concealment of the birth of a child."

There were many loudly voiced concerns over the plight of single mothers. One doctor wrote:

> Above all let, women feel that they should not be visited with so much indignation for simple pregnancy as for murder. Let society, if possible, look on the fact of illegitimate pregnancy with a more forgiving eye, and pity at least the unhappy victims of seduction, or the otherwise innocent who may have fallen. Let such victims have their future course through life of a less hopeless character.

Mr Drury prosecuted for the Crown and Mr Goschen had been asked by the Judge to defend as Bertha had no legal representation. Bertha's mother was called as a witness, but she was in such a distressed state and unable to stand that a chair had to be provided and she wept throughout the trail. Sgt. Stroud stated that any person wishing to travel from the Sevenoaks Union workhouse to Dunton Green would not pass the pond where the baby was found without purposely making a detour. Dr Taylor stated that there were no visible external marks of violence, that the brain vessels were engorged but no sign of disease and the lungs were also healthy and when tested floated in water. He then gave a detailed account of all the other organs before expressing the opinion that death was due to suffocation possibly by the handkerchief.

Mr Drury asked him, 'Suffocation might have been produced by putting a handkerchief in the mouth?'

'Yes.'

The Judge the intervened and asked, 'The handkerchief found would be sufficient to cause suffocation?'

'Yes, my Lord.'

'Is it possible from what you have seen that death may have been caused on November 26th. - you saw it on December 21st?'

'Death might have been caused on November 26th, my Lord.'

The rather desperate defence lawyer asked the doctor, 'Have you ever heard of a case where a child wrapped in a shawl has been suffocated while being carried without the child making any movement to attract the attention of the person carrying it?'

'I don't think a child would be suffocated without making some effort to avoid suffocation.'

'Haven't you heard of cases of overlaying?'

'Yes, when the child is in bed with a mother.'

'You are not sure that death occurred from suffocation?'

'All the signs were of suffocation.'

'Not by drowning?'

'No.'

'In a case where the respiratory organs were partially blocked would it not be likely to produce convulsions in a child?'

'Yes.'

'Would death by convulsions cause suffocation?'

'It would not be improbable, but many of the signs of convulsions would be found in the body.'

'Can you say in this case definitely that death occurred by suffocation and not by convulsions?'

'I should say that the signs I discovered in the post mortem were the signs of suffocation.'

Mr Goschen in his closing speech contended quite ably that there was absolutely no evidence to show that the prisoner wilfully caused the child's death. He suggested that the handkerchief might have got into the child's mouth by accident. If, on the other hand, it was put there by the prisoner, in a culpably negligent manner, that would amount to manslaughter.

The jury took half an hour to convict Bertha of manslaughter rather than murder with a recommendation for mercy. The judge concurred with their verdict and commented that whether the child was hers or not was not a matter that he should take into consideration. The prosecution after further investigation had established that the father of the child was a foreigner who had since left the country. He stated that he could not speak in sufficiently severe terms of this man's conduct. This was, however, no justification for the act that Bertha had committed.

He then looked at Bertha and said, 'I implore you to be more careful in future. Look back on the past and let it be a severe lesson to you. I order you to be imprisoned for twelve month's with hard labour. Edwin and the superintendent were commended by the judge for their diligence.

Bertha survived her twelve-month sentence and on her release moved to Worthing in Sussex where no one knew her and managed to find a job as a servant. She soon found love with John Sheppard, two years younger and a market gardener, and they married in 1909 and set up home in 2 Brougham Cottages, Brougham Road, East Preston just outside Worthing. Daughter Ethel arrived in 1910 and the following year another daughter Maggie. Life was good, but then World War One interrupted their bliss, John went to war and didn't come back. She became a widow with two young children living on a war pension. She died in 1933 aged 46.

4

A Tonbridge Lady Duped (1901)

At the end of the nineteenth century there was a boom in the publication of matrimonial newspapers where both men and women advertised for spouse's and it was a condition that they had to disclose their income to ascertain their financial and social status. This allowed prospective suitors to discover the possible cost of courtship and marriage. Unfortunately it also allowed opportunities for con men or sham lovers to seek out desperate widows and spinsters with money and property ripe for defrauding by professing to be rich bachelors. Matrimonial fraud was common, causing much heartbreak to the victims.

T.H. Rose, a Victorian writer, offered this advice and warning to women:

> This subject I cannot conclude without a caution to females possessed of property. There is always a class of men pretending to be respectable, and who perhaps are so till they have the means of leading a life of idleness and pleasure at the expense of others, and who make it their business, under colour of love, and by the kindest and most diligent

attention, to win your affections, and so to induce you to marry them. But such a man's kindness will at longest but last till he has spent the whole of your property; or which, one way or another, by fraud or violence, he will be sure in the end to plunder you.

*

Annie Maria Chalklin was a rather shy nervous twenty-five-year-old educated lady from a respectable family. She lived with her widowed mother Rebecca, three brothers and a sister at Geneva Villa, a large villa style detached house at 28 Pembury Road, Tonbridge in Kent and the family lived comfortably. This was thanks to her father Francis who had established a profitable brick making factory thanks to the boom in house and infrastructure building. He bequeathed the factory to William his eldest son who became head of the household and was very protective of his two sisters.

She spent a lot of time with her younger sister Edith for companionship and despite her encouragement and help her search for a suitable husband or any husband for that matter had been unsuccessful. Although Annie had a few suitors over the years, spinsterhood loomed. Everyone, including her mother, kept telling her she wasn't getting any younger. Such was her desperation that she had recently resorted to scouring the matrimonial columns of London newspapers for a possible mate. She had kept this secret from her family particularly her mother. She did answer one of the advertisements using the name of Ada Wood and the gentleman did reply to her, but she couldn't summon the nerve to actually meet him. Eventually in March 1901 she perused the personal columns again and spotted one in the *People* newspaper that piqued her interest. This time she showed the advertisement to Edith who had initially giggled about it and embarrassed Annie, but realising her sister's distress told her to answer it and make sure she met the man this time. The advertisement read:

> City gentleman, 34, of good family and social standing, income £800 desires to meet honourable, educated lady; widow not objected to: with a view to early marriage. Write fully in strict confidence. References exchanged. HS. 508. People office. Arundel St, Strand.

Emboldened by Edith's support she wrote a response and once again used the pseudonym of Ada Wood and sent it to the newspaper office. On 22 March she received a reply and excitedly opened it as she rushed up to her bedroom calling her sister. Edith was just as excited and followed her into the bedroom saying, 'Ooh, I wonder what it says. Quickly get it open.' Annie sat on her bed and read the letter.

'He wants to meet me and asks if he can come down from London to see me as soon as possible.'

'How exciting I wonder what he is like. Are you going to meet him?'

'I don't see why not but please don't tell mama or anyone else.'

'I won't, it will be our secret for now,' beamed Edith. 'You must sit down and write back to him.' This she did and an appointment to meet was made, and a week later on 29 March she was standing in the waiting room of Tunbridge Wells station nervously awaiting the London train. She kept a look out for any single man and noticed quite a handsome dapper looking gentleman scouring the waiting room and as their eyes met, he smiled and acknowledged her. Annie smiled back and he approached taking off his hat.

'You must be Miss Chalklin,' he said.

'I am.'

'I am Joseph Everitt Field, the person you have been corresponding with through the post.'

'It is a pleasure to meet you. Please call me Annie.'

'Shall we walk. You must show me this wonderful town that I have heard so much about.'

For the next couple of hours the couple wandered the parks, colonnaded walkways of the Georgian Pantiles and promenaded along the river where Joe told her about his partnership in his father's merchant business and how his father was trying to force him to marry a girl he had chosen for him, but to who he didn't want to marry. He explained that was the reason for his advertisement. Joe told her he had plenty of money and described his cosmopolitan lifestyle travelling to Paris and other parts of Europe on business. It all sounded so thrilling to Annie who was beginning to feel quite taken with him.

Having spent a pleasant afternoon together Annie waved goodbye to him at the station having invited him down to meet her family on Easter Monday, just over a week later which at first he was rather reticent about but eventually agreed. When she got home an excited Edith cornered her demanding to know all that had happened. Annie told her that she had arranged for him to visit on Easter Monday and that she was worried about how her mother and brothers would react. It took her a couple of days to pluck up the courage to tell them and as expected they were not that delighted about her meeting a stranger from an advertisement without telling them. William was particularly disturbed.

Annie had inherited her Auntie's house in Primrose Hill, Tonbridge a few years previously which was rented out and this had caused some recent tensions in the family because William was keen to get hold of some money from it. He had badgered Annie somewhat with the help of his mother over this matter and she was uncertain what to do. She had finally relented and told

William she would consider releasing some money from the property and give it to him as a loan.

When on Easter Monday Joseph arrived in a cab, she was standing at the front door to greet him while the others stood back in the hallway not sure what to expect. Rebecca, her mother, looked the smartly dressed man up and down as he walked towards her and was introduced by Annie and insisted they all call him Joe. He was polite, articulate and well-mannered so on first impressions Rebecca was more relaxed about him but watching him closely during the afternoon she thought him older than he professed to be and perhaps too self-assured. Joe was very forthright to the family and told them to ask him as many questions as they wished. He explained he was a merchant and regaled them with his business plans and travelling. Later while talking to Joe privately in the garden Annie told him about the house and that her mother and brother wanted her to release money from it to give to them. As Joe was a businessman she asked his advice about protecting her money from her relations. Joe said she should seek advice from a solicitor or auctioneer on the best course of action but thought she should sell her reversionary interest in the house.

The rest of the day went well and Edith was charmed by him but William and her mother still had reservations. Later that week she visited the family solicitors Wardley, Barton and Terry at 61 London Road and spoke to William Wardley who agreed that the best course of action to retrieve some money from the house was to sell the reversionary interest in the house.

The relationship blossomed throughout the summer with Joe occasionally visiting Annie, but he always insisted he was too busy with business matters to come regularly. Most of the visits took place when Rebecca and William were not present as the atmosphere was always tense due to their distrust of the prospective son in law. Annie was very smitten with him and became dependent on him. He finally proposed to her romantically in Kew Gardens on a special trip she made to London, but disappointingly for her did not give her a ring, only promising to choose one with her at a later date. Annie was in raptures and immediately accepted his proposal, but her family were still highly wary of the man and William went as far as making enquiries about him in London but could find little information.

Following the engagement in August, Joe became more interested in what her intentions were regarding her house. She informed him that she was considering making some money available to the family. A little while later he referred to the property again and brought down a gentleman friend of his who Annie had never seen before named Mr Mathieson. Joe said he knew all about financial matters and the two of them used their persuasion to advise her to sell it. She had never thought of parting with the property altogether until they convinced her of all the benefits of having all the money on hand. She put the house up for sale in September and Joe rather forcefully insisted that she should not accept any offer without first discussing and getting his consent which should have been a warning to her, but she was too wrapped up in the thought of marriage to worry. She was already gathering her trousseau.

With her house on the market Joe began discussing with Annie where they should live after the wedding and proposed they should live nearer London and that he would search for a suitable house. He filled her with dreams of a large house with servants and her as the mistress. She would laugh at this saying they could not afford it but again he told her he was rich and it wasn't a problem. He continued to keep her posted on the progress of his house hunting over the next few weeks while negotiations over the sale of her house continued throughout October to December during which time Joe made sure he was available to advise her. She soon found a buyer and accepted an offer of £405 through her solicitor, with Joe's consent, at the beginning of December which was not as much as she hoped but Joe had pushed for a quick sale telling her it was best to receive the cash before the marriage. She received the money on Friday 6 December which miraculously coincided with her receiving a letter from Joe postmarked Poste Restante, Paris:

> *My Dearest Annie, I have for some time been looking out for a pretty little villa and I received this morning a letter from a dear friend stating that there is for sale a freehold on a charming place at Teddington situated on the River Thames. They are asking £900 (£135,000) but am told in confidence they will accept £750. What am I to do? Buy or not. Don't fall out with your people but be firm. Best love, Yours ever, Joe.*

It sounded an imposing house, far grander than the villa which he had first suggested as it was, according to him, a freehold ten-bedroom manor house with a coach house, stabling and even a billiard room. Cleverly he had put the onus on her to make the decision on buying the house and fearful her family might dissuade her he mentioned being firm with them. Totally besotted she took the decision to buy the house even though she had not seen any paperwork or had viewed it. She had complete faith in Joe.

He was quick to return to Tonbridge and arrived on Sunday 8 December, and at a family gathering told them that he had arranged for them to get married at Saint Stephen's Church in London on 22 December and said a special licence was to be obtained, although he never made any mention of this on the days leading up to the marriage. He assured Rebecca that they would live comfortably and happily together and told her to arrange a wedding breakfast for which he would pay her later. Once away from the family he told Annie in private that he was going to purchase the house in her name and would arrange for the purchase during the following week, but he explained he only had £500 available at present. This was because he had just purchased a large consignment of bankruptcy stock which had temporarily left him short. This was very plausible at the time as many businesses were going bankrupt and regular special auctions were held where businessmen bought up stock at ridiculously discounted prices to lucratively sell on.

He asked her if she would help him out with £250, pointing out they did not want to lose the fabulous house which she would obviously own. In order to prove to her his means he showed her a bank note with an account number and told her he had £4,000 in it. She believed the house to be in existence and that he was purchasing it, so she readily agreed to loan the money in order to complete the purchase. While they were out for an evening strolling arm and arm, he stopped under a lamppost and retrieved a London and Westminster Bank cheque from his coat pocket which he showed her in the subdued light. It had been filled out to the amount of £842.10 shillings and dated 22 December, drawn and signed by E & R Rhodes and made payable to J Field Esq. He told her it was a wedding gift which he would give her later, and it would be honoured if she put it through her banking account the day before she was married.

He was obviously in a hurry to get matters sorted so he stayed in Tonbridge overnight at a hotel and next morning he collected Annie at ten-thirty, and the couple went to the London and County Bank in town where Annie had an account. At the bank William Valentine Hubbard, the teller, attended to them. Annie asked for a cheque to be made out to Mr Field for £250, but Joe pulled her aside and suggested she gave him £320 to cover other business expenses and to give him the money in cash and gold. Once again she easily agreed although the clerk looked a little quizzical when Joe asked for £300 in bank notes and £20 in gold. The clerk counted out two £50 notes and two £100 notes plus twenty pounds in gold coins. When the clerk pushed the money through the partition Annie moved aside to let Joe take it, but he stood back and nodded for her to accept it which again gave the clerk some concern as it all seemed awkward. Annie put the money in her bag, and they left.

Joe suggested they celebrate by going into the Rose and Crown coaching inn, an imposing Tudor building with a portico entrance crowned with the large royal arms emblem just six doors down the High Street at number 125. Having settled at a table and ordered drinks, he asked for the money and Annie handed it to him. He explained his behaviour at the bank by saying it seemed rather gauche to have taken it in the bank. He then gave her the cheque for £842 ten shillings which was in his pocket. They chatted about their new house and he suggested she should start looking for a good maid and furniture and handed three newspaper advertisements of furniture sales. It all made Annie feel that it was all becoming real and not a dream. They then went into the Telegraph office where he sent off a telegram purporting to agree to purchasing the house. The couple strolled to the railway station and discovered there was quite a wait for the next train to London, so they went into the refreshment room and chatted. During the conversation Joe was showing signs of nervousness and at one-point startled Annie by saying 'Now remember Annie it is best all round if you do not tell your family about the money,' and then added, 'or I will come down and blow your brains out.' He laughed it off as a joke but nevertheless it startled her and then the train screeched to a halt at the platform. Joe said, 'That's all sorted then.

I will contact you about the house and when you can see it and I'll be back soon.' Annie watched as he got into the train, his pocket laden with gold and notes, and waved him off as the train slowly pulled away amidst a cloud of hissing steam. She was beginning to feel uneasy about the whole thing but still had complete faith in her beau.

Annie went home to her family and spent the next couple of days with Edith buying new clothes and wedding attire and eagerly awaiting news from her beloved Joe. By Wednesday she was beginning to worry as at least she had expected a telegram. She went to the telegraph office and sent him one, chiding him for not contacting her and asking why he did not keep his promise to contact her about the house. Again no immediate response so she telegraphed him again and this time she received the perplexing reply: *'Am leaving for Algiers. Stop. Urgent. Stop Writing. Joe'*

A short letter followed sent from the West Strand post office in London which reduced her to tears and sent her running to find her mother:

> *I only arrived this morning. I fear to my extreme regret that I shall not see Christmas in England. The cheque I gave you I forgot to endorse. Kindly send it to me that I may do so as soon as possible. I am bringing things to a successful conclusion and hope to please you very much. I am on a good thing but cannot tell you yet. Love, Yours, Joe.*

Annie was distraught as the only reason she had agreed to give him money was his promise to marry her and to buy the house. It now appeared that he not only intended cancelling the wedding but had run off to Algiers. The family rallied round calling Joe a cad and a criminal. She did not see Joe again until he was arrested.

*

William and her mother were now convinced that there was something badly wrong and pleaded with Annie to go to the police, but she refused to leave her room and just sat sobbing while the family tried to convince her. Eventually Annie went to Tonbridge police station on the 16 December to report that she believed she had been defrauded. She was eventually interviewed by the Tonbridge Divisional Superintendent Robert Styles. Having heard the story he organised a warrant for the arrest of Joe. He realised this was a case for Edwin and his newly formed detective department in as it would involve a great deal of investigation. He sent a message to him and he travelled to Tonbridge by train with detective constable Petley.

On being appraised of the details of the case Edwin immediately began his investigations by visiting the London and County bank who had issued the notes and speaking to the cashier and chief clerk, Herbert Reinherdt Schonan and also William Valentine Hubbard in charge of the bank's ledger. They managed to obtain the serial numbers of the notes they had issued which were 72381 and 13867 for the two £50 notes and 20800 and 64239 for the two £100 notes and each one was stamped with the bank's logo.

Edwin passed these serial numbers to New Scotland Yard on the 17 December. Det. Sgt. Francis Carline was given the task of visiting the Bank of England where he retrieved the notes all bearing the stamp of the London and County Bank in Tonbridge. One note for £100 had been used to open an account at the London, City and Midland Bank in Manchester in the name of Stanley Stamford and the others used to open an account at the Charing Cross branch of the London, City and Midland Bank in London.

Bank notes for large amounts of money were a rarity in that period and mainly used in commerce for large transactions if the use of a cheque wasn't possible. Most of the general public used coins and notes of small value. Individual banks when required would issue their own stamped bank notes with a serial number either for a specific amount or a set amount. They were literally 'notes' telling a person the bank would honour the payment. The printing of bank notes began in 1855 with a £5 note, but mass printing came much later. When issued or cashed the banks would make a note of the transaction in their ledgers so it was possible to track when and where a note was used.

Carline reported back to Edwin his findings and he decided it was time to make a trip to London to follow up the leads. He began the paper trail by visiting the London City and Midland Bank in Charing Cross where he spoke to the manager John Edward Marsden. He gave him the serial numbers of the notes and asked if he could trace when they were cashed and if the bank had heard of Joseph Field. The manager gave the numbers to his senior ledger clerk and Edwin sat talking with the manager until the clerk returned. He told Edwin that some of the notes had been used to open an account under the name of Joseph Aintree Verney. John had dealt with the transaction being a new account, and a large sum of money and remembered it well and of talking to the gentleman. He had told him that he had just arrived from Paris and had come to London to start a business and was staying at the expensive Charing Cross Hotel. He produced a reference from a Mr Yule Stanton, of 22 Rue Venars, Passy, Paris. Mr Marsden told him he accepted the account subject to their inquiries being satisfactory.

'How much did he pay into the account?' Edwin asked.

'He paid in a total of £220, made-up of a £100 note, two £50 notes and £20 in gold coins. I take it officer that the man has been up to no good?'

'You could say that.'

'I had my suspicions at the time, but he came in the next day and introduced a man named Yule Stanton who had given him the reference so I gave him a chequebook.'

'When was this?'

'On Wednesday 11 December he paid in £10 and used the cheque book three times for two withdrawals of £10 and one for £13 which the bank honoured.'

'And you say you were not impressed with this Mr Verney.'

'I felt he presented himself as being very much like a Drury Lane villain,' sniffed the manager.

'And you were right sir. So we are now missing a £100 note.'

Next stop was the Charing Cross Post Office where Walter Rice, the counter clerk informed him that on 9 December a man came in and tendered a £100 note in payment for a £10 money order to Paris payable to a Mr Yule Stanton the senders name being J Field, and he gave the man £90 change. The remaining £100 Tonbridge note had been cashed in Manchester and Edwin immediately contacted the Manchester police giving them a description and asking their assistance in tracking down the wanted Joe.

While Edwin was waiting for news from Manchester police Annie's family pressured him about the £842 London and Westminster cheque that Joe had given Annie, and which was still in her possession. They did not know what to do with it or whether it was genuine. Eventually Edwin agreed to accompany William to London to track down the veracity of the cheque. The London and Westminster bank was situated in Mincing Lane, in the City of London, and linked Fenchurch Street and Great Tower Street. Edwin had not frequented the area before and he was fascinated as the lane was the centre of the tea and spice trade and they passed by the famous magnificent two storey London Commercial Salerooms where the goods were auctioned. The bank was expecting them, and they were introduced to Arthur Folliott Hancock the ledger keeper who kept the massive bound ledgers which contained all of the bank's transactions. Edwin handed him the cheque and he searched their records. It took him sometime but declared eventually that they had no record of ever having an account under the name of Rhodes or Field and if the cheque had been presented it would not have been cashed. It was a fake.

*

On December 20 Edwin received a telegram from Manchester police informing him they had Joe in custody. They had gone to the bank where the £100 cheque had been cashed and the staff were able to tell them that Joe was staying at the expensive and imposing Royal Hotel in Manchester. Several officers had rushed to the hotel, but Joe wasn't there, so they laid in wait in the foyer until he walked in and was pointed out by the concierge. The surprised Joe gave himself up without a struggle pleading his innocence to any wrong and bewildered about the reason for his arrest. On receiving the news Edwin travelled by train to Manchester with Det Constable George Fisher to arrest Joe. They were met at Manchester Central railway station and taken to the police station.

On arrival he took Joe into an interview room who told him there must be a mistake as his name was Joseph Austen Verning trading as Austen and Stanley not Field. Edwin would have none of it and charged him under the names of Verning alias Field. The charge was "making certain false pretences to Annie Maria Chalklin, daughter of the late Mr Frank Chalklin of Primrose Hill Tonbridge on the 9 December and other dates and thereby unlawfully and knowingly obtaining from her the sum of £320 with intent to cheat and defraud.'

Realising he had been found out Joe replied, 'I had no intention to defraud her of £300. If she had waited I would have paid her back £400 within a month. I had written to her saying I was on to an excellent thing and had opened offices at 46 and 47 Atlantic Chambers in Paris to trade under my new Company of Austen and Stanhope. I was leaving on Thursday or Friday next for Paris to open the office there. I had opened a banking account at the Market Street branch of the London City and Midland Bank, and I had intended to work the three offices together.'

'What a web of lies you have managed to weave with all your various names, companies and accounts.'

'All legitimate sir.'

'Come now, we know the whole thing is a sham including the bogus love affair.'

Then Joe astounded Edwin by telling him that he was already married.

'So you are telling me that your intention was to commit bigamy?'

'Well kind of.'

'There is no kind of. I would say you were a bit of a cad sir.'

'That's your opinion but I maintain my innocence as an upright businessman. I would have given the money back with interest once the trading had begun.'

'But an innocent man doesn't take money from a lady, falsely propose marriage, plan to commit bigamy and then travel round the country opening accounts under false names.'

'It is all a misunderstanding, I assure you.'

'Do you not realise that you have ruined the young lady's reputation, caused her heartbreak, embarrassment, and made her ill?'

'If that is so I am sorry, but there was no intention on my part of causing this.'

Edwin thanked the Manchester police for their quick and efficient tracking down of Joe and apprehending him. He and George then handcuffed him and escorted him to Manchester station and made the long journey via London to Tonbridge during which he gave them no trouble and continually made denials of any wrong doing and expounded on his business plans. Once in Tonbridge he was placed in a cell awaiting his appearance at the police court in front of the magistrates and then looked into Joe's claim to be already married.

Prior to the court case Edwin was able to confirm that while Joe was meeting with Annie at the end of March he was also courting another lady in London who he had also promised to marry and worse still while he was encouraging Annie to sell her house he had gone through with the marriage by licence on 13 June to 56-year-old widow Frances Taylor under the name Joseph Pope Field at Saint Martins in the Fields church in Charing Cross. On the night before they had both stayed at the Craven Hotel 43-46 Craven Street in the Strand at her expense. Joe did like to live the high life. Joe's alleged father Thomas Field listed as a merchant was present and the bride's father William Parker, a retired army officer also. Edwin spoke to Richard Bennett, the Vestry Clerk to confirm this and he later identified Joe saying he had a good memory of all the faces of persons who came into the church to be married.

*

The first magistrates hearing was held on Saturday 21 December at the Tonbridge Police Court part of the police station in Pembury Road with C Fitch Kemp Esq. and W Baldwin Esq. on the bench. Edwin had been at the police station early talking with Supt Styles about the case and they had wandered to the court foyer together. They watched Joe Field being escorted into the court.

The smartly dressed and rather bemused and arrogant Joseph Everett Field alias Verney of 60 Queen Victoria St. City, London sauntered into the court and stood in the dock. The clerk read the charge of making certain false pretences to Annie Maria Chalklin of Genoa Villa Primrose Hill Tonbridge on the 9 December and other dates.

Mr Percival Hughes barrister rose to open the case on behalf of the prosecution and was accompanied and instructed by Annie's solicitors, Messrs Reston and Cardell of Claremont House. He began by stating, 'I have no wish to prejudice the accused, but this was a heartless fraud on the poor girl from whom he obtained this money by false pretences. Unfortunately the conduct of the prisoner has led to the entire collapse of the lady who is unable to be present.'

Mr Fitch Kemp, the chairman, asked, 'Then we may take it that the lady is not able to be present owing to ill-health?'

'That is so, and I have medical evidence,' replied Mr Hughes.

Joe Field then interjected,' I have nothing to say against this young lady, but I am somewhat prejudiced, as my legal adviser, who has been telegraphed for from London, has not yet arrived. Owing to his non-arrival I would deem it a great favour if you would permit me to have a small piece of pencil and paper to take notes?'

The Clerk replied, 'Certainly,' and handed them to him.

Percival Hughes then called Dr Isaac Newton.

'I am Miss Chalkin's doctor and have been attending her and last saw her yesterday.'

'Can you give an indication when she might be able to attend court?' asked the chairman.

'I would say that she might be able to attend in a week or a fortnight.'

'But the bench day is Tuesday,' announced the Clerk. 'She could not attend so soon as Tuesday.'

A suave Joseph Field in court.

British Newspaper Archive

'But she might?' asked the rather uncompassionate Clerk.

The Chairman spoke to the Doctor, 'Are you saying she might have a temporary relapse?

Joe Field then started speaking, 'I am very sorry for the young lady is unwell, as I have great respect for her.'

The Chairman gave him a glare and then the Clerk continued, 'Don't you think that in a week she may recover?'

'She may, but it is not always easy to speak of a nervous case.'

Mr Hughes then made a plea to the Chairman, 'Would it be convenient to the Bench to take the case this day week. The doctor has some doubt as to the state of her mind, and the evidence will have to be very carefully given?'

The Chairman looked to his colleague who nodded and said, 'I shall be willing to take the case this day week, looking to the doctor's evidence.'

This having been agreed upon, Mr. Hughes said he would state some of the facts of the case, but before he could begin Joe shouted, 'This is not justice, Sir, please, I am undefended.'

'Mr Field I cannot put up with these outbursts. You have plenty of time to make sure your solicitor is present next time.'

Mr Hughes then gave an outline of the case mentioning that Field had given Annie a cheque for £842 drawn from the account of a bankrupt man on which the police might bring another charge. Also that that the prisoner had been travelling round the continent in association with another man and that the prisoner had done an extraordinary thing for an innocent man by opening an account in a false name.

The Chairman intervened at this point and advised,' I merely want evidence sufficient to justify a remand. I don't want you to go into the detailed particulars of the case.'

Edwin was then called and entered the court and stood in the witness box. He gave his account of how he had received the warrant and made initial investigations. He stated he had traced the money from the Tonbridge bank to several London banks where they were cashed and some of the money paid into an account under the names of Verning and Everett Stanley. He had tracked down the prisoner to various hotels including the London Paris Hotel in Newhaven and finally to the Royal Hotel in Manchester where he discovered two cheques had been cashed at a bank. From the description given by all the interviews he ascertained it was Field and apprehended the prisoner who insisted his name was Joseph Austen Verning and that he was a legitimate businessman trading as Austen and Stanley. Edwin charged him as Verning alias Field.

Edwin then got out his notebook opened it and said, 'the prisoner in reply to the warrant "I had no intention of defrauding….."

At this point Joe shouted, 'This is not justice sir, please. I am undefended.

Mr Hughes told Edwin, 'Put your notes away.'

Edwin then continued, 'He said "I had no intention of defrauding her of the £300. I would have paid her back £400 within a month. I was on to a good thing and had opened offices in Manchester and Paris."

The Clerk then stopped Edwin, 'We had better leave it there.'

Joe then asked Edwin, 'I gave you no trouble whatever, and offered every information?'

Edwin replied, 'Yes, that is true. You told me you were a married man, and everything.'

'All about the bank account and what it was?'

'Yes.'

The Clerk asked Joe, 'Have you any objection to a remand?'

'Yes, I do. I had no intention of defrauding this girl. I must express my regret at the illness of the young lady. My legal advisor has not arrived, but in granting a remand I would ask you to consider the question of bail. Had the money been asked for it would have been paid back and will be paid back in twenty-four hours.'

The clerk responded, 'So you have nothing to say why you should not be remanded until next Saturday, but you ask to be given bail?'

Yes, sir,' replied Joe.

There was an audible gasp from Styles and Edwin and both jumped up and Styles could not stop himself from angrily addressing the magistrates.

'With all due respect sirs, I must strongly object to any thought of giving this man bail.'

'I have a complete answer to the charge,' shouted Joe.

Mr Hughes interjected and agreed stating, 'I don't want to be hard on the man, but it is a very serious charge, and the prisoner has been travelling about all over the place including France and the continent so I must concur with the police officers.'

After a discussion with his colleague the chairman addressed the court, 'We disagree as to the chances of the prisoner absconding but will set a substantial sum £500 from yourself and two sureties of £250 which must satisfy the police.'

Joe was taken to the cells and later escorted by Edwin to Maidstone prison pending the bail arrangements being satisfied.

*

The second magistrates hearing convened a week later on Saturday 28 December and this time his solicitor did turn up. He was represented by Mr C Tyndale Davis instructed by Mr C.J. Pridham of 83 Finsbury Pavement London EC.

This time Annie was suitably recovered to give evidence so much so that on stepping into the witness box she fixed her gaze on Field in the dock, taking no interest in everything around her as though in a trance. It was a classic scenario of if looks could kill and a woman scorned. When the clerk gently spoke to her his voice finally brought her back to reality. She still seemed to be suffering from shock. The clerk passed the bible to her, and she took the oath in a faint voice. Mr Percival Hughes barrister was again prosecuting and rose to open the case and began laying out the case in detail:

> 'In March last, by some means, which he understood was through the press, the prisoner and the lady became acquainted. The prisoner afterwards came down from London and visited her at her house, where everything was perfectly regular, and he became engaged to her. It was known to some of the family that he had not only become engaged, but that it had been arranged that on December 22 the marriage would take place. He had promised all along to marry her and it was this, and the purchase of the house which induced her to part with the money. If he had not telegraphed he was going to Algiers she would not have taken out the warrant.
>
> They had now discovered since the arrest that he was a married man, and therefore that might to some extent explain the collapse of the lady. The charge was one of false pretences and he would put into the box Detective Sergeant Fowle who would tell them that having received a warrant for the prisoner's arrest, he eventually discovered him in Manchester.
>
> It appeared that on December 9 the prisoner came down to Tonbridge to see to see the lady. She was getting every-

thing ready for the wedding. The prisoner represented that he was attaining a certain house, mentioning the locality and describing the premises, and the house was supposed to be on the bank of the River Thames near Teddington. This being so, she went with him to the London & County Bank at Tonbridge and having an interest in certain monies deposited there she withdrew with the prisoner there and under his influence £320 from her account. She took the money and handed it to the prisoner, in return for which he gave her a cheque for £843.10 shillings drawn by G.J Rhodes on the London & Westminster Bank. There would also be false pretences with reference to that cheque for it has been found that no such account existed, and withdrawn from the account of a bankrupt gentleman, and will be found in evidence that this was grounds upon which the prisoner will be given another charge. It is a very serious charge. Indeed, one which would probably require a week's remand over and above the present one, as it would be necessary for him to bring witnesses from the several banks to show them the character of the fraud.

The prisoner had been travelling about on the continent in association with another man. Having obtained the money, the prisoner did a thing extraordinary for an innocent man to do. He went and banked the money in a false name in the London City & Midland Bank in London instead of buying the house. He took £100 to the Charing Cross Post Office, took an order for £10 and sent it on to the man whose name will be mentioned later on in the case.'

Annie was then examined by Joe's solicitor, Mr Tindall Davis who gave her a long and quite aggressive cross examination. He began by asking her what property she had interest in, and she told him the family home and a house in primrose Hill left to her brother William, her sister and two other brothers. Then Mr Davis asked: 'Has your brother William or mother at any time induced you, or tried to induce you, to part with any portion of your reversionary interest?'

Mr. Hughes objected to the question as being totally irrelevant to the case at issue, which was solely one of false pretences stating 'How the property came into the possession of Annie had nothing whatever to do with the case.'

Mr Davis assured the bench that he had good grounds in the interests of the prisoner's defence to ask the question and was allowed to continue.

'I need to ask you again whether your brother William or mother at any time induced you to part with any portion of your interest in the house?'

Annie was in quite a nervous state at this point and her answer was almost inaudible, so the Chairman asked her to speak more loudly. She then answered and again it was inaudible, so the Clerk encouraged her to speak up and she finally replied 'no.'

Mr Davis continued, 'Did you tell Mister Field that your brother William and your mother had tried to get all your property out of you?'

Annie replied, 'I told him they wanted some money.'

Mr Davis persisted, 'Did you not tell him that you wished to protect your money from your relatives?'

Annie replied hesitantly, 'Yes, I did but it was under his advice.'

Mr Davis asked, 'Did you not make the first suggestion?'

'I told him how I stood, and he suggested I should protect myself.'

'You gave this money to him on the 9th. and on the 21st. he was arrested. Now, do you think that was sufficient time for him to have purchased this house?'

'He telegraphed he was going to Algiers.'

'Was there any attempt made to get a licence?'

'He suggested he would do it himself.'

'Had you any reason to doubt that he intended to purchase this house in Teddington?'

'No, I had no reason to doubt him at the time.'

'Have you any reason now to believe that he would not have completed the purchase if he had time?'

'I don't think he would have done.'

'Why? What makes you think so?'

'Because I have since heard that he is married. When I parted with the money I believed he would marry me and purchase the house.'

Mr Davis then sat down and Annie's mother Rebecca testified that when Joe first came to her house he described himself as a merchant of some sort and there had been no mention of a marriage but on the 8 December he told her 'I am going to marry Annie and I think we can live happily and comfortably together.' They were to be married on the 22 December, and he would make all the arrangements. He had been quite explicit that she must provide the wedding breakfast, and he would pay her. It was only at this point that she was told how they met. She had no idea her daughter desired to protect her money from the family and she had no money from her daughter or tried to persuade her to give her brother any.

Mr Valentine Hubbard, the ledger clerk at the Tonbridge London & County bank gave evidence as did Mr Herbert Schonan the cashier, John Marsham, manager of Charing Cross London City and Midland Bank, Arthur Hancock ledger clerk at Mincing Lane London and Westminster bank and Walter Rice of the Charing Cross Post Office who provided the paper trail of the money obtained by Edwin.

Edwin was called along with Det. Sgt. Francis Carline of New Scotland Yard to give details of tracking the money and the arrest. Richard Bennett, the vestry clerk at Martin-in-the-fields confirmed that Joe was the man who married Frances Taylor on June 13, 1901, six months prior to proposing marriage to Annie and when Mr Davis queried the identification the vestry clerk replied, 'I have a good recollection of all faces of persons who come to my church to be married.'

Mr Davis in his eloquent closing speech maintained that the money had always been a loan and that there were two allegations against the prisoner namely that he obtained this £320 first on the promise of marriage and secondly that he represented he was purchasing a house for them to live in when married. With regard to the cheque for £842.10 shillings it was impossible for the prosecution to prove false pretence for an act of false pretence must be based on something past or present, and not on something future. In regard to the promise to marry, the prosecution has produced several letters, but there was not one word in writing about this suggested promise, even though the prisoner corresponded for nine months from March to December. Joe visited the mother's house but there was no real talk about marriage, and there had been no engagement ring. There was nothing to bear out this promise or that it was on this pretence alone that she loaned him this money, but she had specifically stated that this money was a loan. The prosecution could not suddenly turn a loan into a charge of false pretence, where there was no proof that the person having the loan did not intend to return it within a given time.

There was not the slightest doubt that the prisoner had a house in view, that the bargain would have been completed, and that the prisoner would have had her money returned if Joe had been given reasonable time. This money was purely a loan, and the prisoner had offered to return the whole of the money, as the Detective Sergeant had said, and he was still willing at once to do this. How could you commit a man to prison on the evidence of a woman who made a pastime of answering matrimonial advertisements. He asked the bench why on such bare testimony as had been adduced, commit the prisoner for trial on one of the greatest offences in the annals of their criminal law.

Mr Davis asked the bench that the prisoner preferred that he should be sent to the Assizes rather than the Quarter Sessions in order that the defence might be more adequately prepared. Mr Davis still insisted that there was no prima facie case made out to warrant the magistrates sending it before a judge and jury. Mr Hughes raised no objection to the case being delayed until the Assizes.

The magistrates declared there was a case to answer, and Joe replied, "I plead not guilty and reserve my defence." He was committed for trial at the next Assizes. and bail continued at £500 with two sureties of £250. They had been in session for five and a half hours.

*

At the Kent Winter Assizes on Saturday 22 February Joseph Hope Field was described in court by Mr Dickens, K.C., the prosecutor as 'not a very nice person or of good character, but had the looks, flair, charm and patter which attracted women and proved an asset.'

He pleaded guilty and being ever the gentleman declared he was willing to do this "in order to save Miss Chaklin any further annoyance and inconvenience." His defence lawyer insisted this was done out of sincere motives and contrition for his past conduct. Judge Wright did not fall for his patter and sentenced him to 3 years hard labour.

By the time the Assizes convened the full extent of his criminal life and penchant for seducing women was now fully exposed, thus the plea of guilty. Joseph Field alias Ralph made his first appearance in court at the age of twenty-two at the Old Bailey on the 23 June 1884. He was charged with bigamy and received six months hard labour. He did not learn his lesson and married again in 1892 and after a few months deserted her to live with another woman whose furniture he stole. He was sentenced in 1898 to twenty-two months of hard labour for this. His wife sued him for adultery and cruelty and obtained a decree nisi which became absolute in July 1899. Undeterred he courted and hoodwinked a wealthy spinster named Matilda Salmon and married her in September 1900. Over the next few months he managed to convince her to sell much of her property and obtained £850 from her before decamping with the proceeds, only to return later full of excuses and managing to part her from more of her property. He eventually deserted her and investigations for a possible charge were ongoing..

At the same time he had already been courting and captivating another lady, a fifty-six-year-old widow named Mrs Frances Taylor who he married at St Martins in Field parish church by licence on June 13. He was thirty-nine at the time. When Annie answered his advert in March 1901 he was still defrauding these two other women.

As for Annie she only managed to retrieve £198 of her money. Judge Wright waived any charges for bigamy as Joseph had not actually married her. Sadly it appears she never found true love or trusted a man after that and she left Tonbridge and began caring for the less fortunate becaming a matron at the Duxhurst Farm Colony for Inebriates and later in her dotage was a companion servant during the war to a aged Jenny Sinden. Annie died aged 88 in 1964 still single.

5

No Way to Treat Your Gardener

On Saturday morning 7 September Edwin was at his desk in his office at the Wrens Cross headquarters completing paperwork on another case when he was handed a telegram addressed to Chief Constable He read it and immediately asked his office clerk to take it to Edwin with a note that he was to take charge of the case and head to Meopham at once to investigate the strange request. Having read the Chief's note he opened the telegram intrigued:

> Can you send a detective to take charge of intended murderer at Meopham with two accomplices. Scotland Yard referred me to you. If so will meet him at the Coppice, Meopham tonight or tomorrow. Ledward.

'What on earth is this?' he exclaimed to himself. He had dealt with some strange events in his career but never seen a telegram like this.

'Take charge of an intended murderer and two accomplices,' he read again, 'None of this sounds real. Could be a hoax I suppose, but better safe than sorry. I may need backup on this one.'

The trouble was he had no other detectives available and the Chief had ordered at once. Meopham village was some twelve miles to the northwest of Maidstone on the North Downs and it would take him a good hour to get there. Before leaving he sent an urgent message to the nearest uniformed police to send back up for him and arranged to meet them at the end of the road where the telegram sender lived.

Thomas Ledward was in fact a retired civil engineer who had done well for himself but now lived in relative seclusion in a sizeable house with a charming garden in The Coppice in the Kent village. On arrival he was thankful to find a Sergeant Saunders and Constable Wood waiting for him.

'Strange one this, eh Inspector?'

'You're right there. Do you know this chap at all.'

'No. We have no record of any dealings with him. We have made a few discreet inquiries while we waited for you with neighbours and passersby and they all knew him.'

'That doesn't sound good.'

'Yeh, a right strange one by all counts.'

'Is he dangerous?'

'More a case of being off his trolley, than anything else by the sounds of it. Apparently he does own guns and often lets them off in the garden. And he's a drinker.'

'Great it gets better and better. Best be careful then.'

They went cautiously through the garden gate up to the back door of the house and knocked loudly. There was no answer so they tried several more times to no avail. Constable Wood tried the front door but the door was locked as was the back door. All three officers looked through the windows to try and spot any signs of life and then wandered the garden, but it was obvious no one was at home.

'Well that's a bit of an anti-climax and a wasted journey,' said a frustrated Edwin.

Edwin left a note on the door saying he would return early in the morning. Next morning it was an early Sunday start and he was at the house at 7.30am and met up with Sergeant Saunders again. This time they had better luck and the door was answered by a dishevelled and drowsy elderly man.

The man stared at Edwin through bleary blood shot eyes and then glanced at the uniformed Sergeant and asked, 'Are you Detective Inspecter Fowle?'

'I am sir. Are you Thomas Ledward?' Edwin responded.

'Yes.'

'I am here in response to your telegram to the Chief Constable.'

'Good, good. Now we are getting somewhere. Come in. Come in,' Ledward said stepping back into the hallway. He led them into the study.

'Take a seat officers.'

'Thank you.'

Once seated Ledward said, 'I'll very soon explain my case to you. I've got all the evidence written out for you. First, Doctor Griffiths the local doctor wants to poison me by giving me an overdose of morphia.'

'Why should he want to do that?' interrupted Edwin.

'Well obviously to steal my will, destroy it, forge another and make the whole of my property over to himself.'

Edwin glanced at the sergeant with raised eyebrows. 'What has given you that impression sir. Sounds very drastic to me?'

'I just know. There is a conspiracy to get my money. He's not acting alone either.'

'I see, he's got accomplices then?'

'Definitely. I suspect Blackman is in on it and the woman Peggy.'

'And who is this Blackman?'

'My gardener of course. Meant to keep my garden looking trim, but a very untrustworthy sort you know. Doesn't know his place.'

'And Peggy?'

'She's the lady I live with.'

'So let me get this straight. You believe, the doctor, the gardener and your companion are all conspiring to kill you and make off with your estate?'

'Quite so. There we have it. I expect you to arrest them right now if you please.'

'Well obviously I cannot just arrest them without any kind of proof.'

'Why not, you have my word on it?'

'It doesn't work like that I am afraid. I shall need to make some enquiries first.'

'You'll find I am right,' said the obviously disappointed Ledward.

Edwin and the sergeant got up and as they exited the house Ledward said, 'Mind you, if there's any compromising over this I will shoot them.'

Edwin turned to look at Ledward and gave him his best glare, 'I don't think you should be talking like that sir. Particularly in front of two police officers.'

As they walked down the lane Edwin said to the sergeant, 'I think you had better keep an eye on him while I find out more.'

'I certainly will sir.'

The following day Edwin tracked down William Edward Blackman the gardener and also spoke to Dr. Griffiths and Mr Miles the landlord of the Green Man pub and from what he could gather from them there was no truth in the accusations. They all agreed Ledward was an eccentric bordering on being mentally unstable through his fondness for drink and drugs. Edwin decided to let the matter rest there.

*

Four days later on Wednesday Blackman was at work as usual tending the garden when at about noon an argument broke out between him and his employer over a glass of beer. Ledward had earlier asked him to get a glass of beer from Blackman's nearby cottage as he had exhausted his own supply. He had duly done this and taken it into Ledward's conservatory and returned to his work. He noticed that his employer was worse for wear and still wearing his pyjamas and rather belligerent which was no surprise and something that he was getting fed up with. A little later Ledward accosted the gardener telling him that the beer was bitter and he had spat it out and accused him of putting something in it.

Soon after he confronted Blackman again demanding to know why he had brought him a beer from the cottage having completely forgotten in his stupor that he had asked for it and drunk it. He then wanted to know why the empty glass had been left in his conservatory to which the gardener tried to explain that he had not had a chance to remove it. By now the gardener was not only fed up with his employer's erratic behaviour but was also concerned. Ledward asked Blackman to go into the conservatory and to wait inside while he entered the back door of the house and reappeared from the dining room door. He shouted at Blackman about the glass again accusing him of putting morphia in it. The stupefied gardener tried to explain again the circumstances of the glass being there.

Ledward then ordered Blackman to take a note to Mr Miles, the landlord of the Green Man pub in the village and he set off walking to the pub. When he got there he explained that his employer, who was well known to Miles who supplied him with most of his beer and alcohol, was in one of his moods and wanted to see him straight away. He told him he was rather worried about his mental state so the landlord accompanied him back to the Coppice. When they got there Ledward greeted Miles, apologised for his night attire and asked him into the conservatory where he ordered some cigars and then ranted on about Blackman and the glass which he believed had been spiked in some way.

Ledward told Miles he would send a note to local constable Hampshire about it and Miles tried to calm him as he was now in a rage and was threatening to go upstairs and get something to sort out Blackman. Minutes later Ledward appeared carrying a cane in one hand and a sword stick in the other and went outside in a rage shouting to Blackman, 'You don't want me to soil my hands on you, do you?'

A startled Blackman replied, 'If you think you can use the cane on me, do so.'

Ledward walked up to him and then whacked the side of his head with the stick knocking him backwards. Miles tried to intervene and pull Ledward away but he would having none of it. The gardener rubbed his bleeding head and jumped at his tottering employer, easily knocking him over and they rolled about on the lawn until Blackman got on top of him and grappled the weapons from Ledward's hands. He got up threw them into the bushes and offered his hand to Ledward to pull him to his feet calmly saying to him, 'Now sir, if you're a man, let's use our fists.

He pulled Ledward up and struck him a heavy blow to his jaw knocking him down again and walked away. Ledward looked up at Miles and said, 'I wouldn't soil my hands to fight him, but I did thrash him with a stick.'

Miles then left and soon after Blackman left the garden and started walking up the lane cursing his mad idiot employer. He had walked about four hundred yards down the lane when he heard a gunshot and a bullet whistled past. He crouched down and turned to see Ledward standing in the lane by the garden gate waving a revolver about and shouting. Blackman started running for his life and reached another fifty yards when another shot rang out and he ducked again. He set off after Miles and reached the pub where the police were called.

Sitting at his desk late that afternoon it was a case of deja'vu for Edwin when he received a message from the Chief requesting him to return to Meopham to make an arrest as there had been a serious incident to deal with. It was nearly 9pm when he finally reached Ledward's house having interviewed Blackman and Miles and obtained an arrest warrant. He knocked on the door accompanied by a detective and Sergeant Saunders and arrested Ledward on a warrant. When he read the warrant Ledward appeared unperturbed and laughed and replied, 'I did say if there's any compromising I will shoot them, and I meant it.' The officers searched the house and found several loaded guns and revolvers which they confiscated.

It was obvious to Edwin that Ledward was not of sound mind so he got in touch with Dr. Herbert J Bryan the police surgeon who gave him a thorough examination in his cell and established that Ledward took large doses of four to six grains of morphia a day and was addicted. Although he was lucid and rational when examined, the doctor diagnosed that he was obviously suffering from drug induced delusions regarding Dr. Griffiths and the others trying to poison him. Dr Bryan said he had no choice but to continue giving him morphine in much smaller doses while in custody to begin weaning him off the drug otherwise he would suffer withdrawal symptoms and might get violent.

Edwin passed all the case information to the Divisional Superintendent A. E. Rhodes whose area the crime was committed as was protocol and he presented the case at Chatham Police Court on Friday 20 September. Ledward was charged with using threats towards Blackman. Supt. Rhodes informed the bench that there was some question as to the state of the prisoner's mind and Dr. Bryan thought it advisable that the prisoner should be detained and kept under observation which they noted. Ledward did his best in court to pass the blame of his actions onto his doctor and was extremely disgruntled that Dr Bryan had reduced his morphia and challenged him in the witness box stating, 'You reduced the dose from six to one grams which was a cruel thing to do. Any other doctor would say so. Didn't I tell you I took the morphia to cure the family habit of taking alcoholic drink like whisky and brandy, and that it succeeded?'

'You did,' replied Dr. Bryan.

'Didn't I tell you that to cut anyone short might bring on delirium tremens?'

'Yes.'

'You gave it me with great reluctance?'

'Yes.'

'Didn't you ask me if I take cocaine?'

'You told me you had done so.'

'It was cruel, most cruel, a most abominable thing to do; to stop it.'

Having heard all the evidence the magistrates retired to make a verdict and decided to adjourn the case for a week to allow for more medical evidence. When they informed Ledward of their decision he immediately asked for bail stating, 'I have £600 in my Gravesend bank account and am more than willing to put this up as security.'

'I'm afraid the seriousness of your offence does not allow us to sanction such a course of action.'

'Do I understand that I am to remain under restraint for a week?' he blustered.

'That is the decision of this court.'

'I am not in the habit of living in a police cell. I don't like it. I have done nothing wrong,' he declared insulted.

'Well in that case we can refer you to the Workhouse.'

'The workhouse!' he exploded astonished, 'I haven't heard anything so stupid. I have never been inside a workhouse in my life. Can't I go to a hotel? You can send half a dozen men there to guard me, and I will pick up the cost.'

The Chairman obviously amused, waved to the lock up keeper to have the still protesting Ledward removed. He was taken to the workhouse, but his erratic behaviour led to him being further examined and certified as insane so he was committed to the Barming lunatic asylum just outside Maidstone. The charges against him were then withdrawn. Two years later he was released and indignant at the way he had been treated in England, booked passage to Canada where he died two years later.

6

The Hythe Canal Mystery (1903)

On the sunny and warm afternoon of 13 July 1903 George Edward Drury left his house at 8 Mount Street in the seaside town of Hythe after finishing his lunch and walked the hundred yards or so to the tow path of the Royal Military canal. The twenty-eight-mile canal was built between 1804 and 1809 between Seabrook near Folkestone and Cliff End near Hastings as a defence against the possible invasion by Napolean and served as a supply route for the army. The canal runs through the middle of the town of Hythe parallel to the High Street. George worked as a water bailiff on the canal for the South East and Central Railway Company. He loved his job particularly in the summer months when he was out and about enjoying the fresh air watching the barges being pulled through and spotting the abundant wildlife.

He was wandering along the south tow path heading west and went past the Twiss Road bridge which connected the High Street to the beach. About twenty yards past the bridge he spotted a brown paper parcel floating on the water. He thought the object must have fallen off one of the barges which was common, and he used his stick to bring the parcel to the bank wondering what it could be. He got on his knees and lifted it out of the water and as he placed it onto the bank, what he thought was a baby's head, poked out causing him to recoil and fall back. Cursing at his stupidity as he realised it must be a doll he crouched and looked closer. To his horror he realised he had been right the first time. It was a baby, and he fell back again in revulsion and shock. After a minute or so when he had calmed down he steeled himself to take another look and realised the baby was dead. He looked around but could see no one else on the tow path or any barges who could help. He left the baby's body on the bank and walked quickly up Twiss Road to the High Street and luckily came across P.C Wills, a local policeman. They hurried back to the tow path where P.C. Wills carried it and took it to the local mortuary. There he carefully opened the package and examined the body looking for any clue to its identification. All he could find was a laundry label on the Turkish towelling the baby was wrapped in with the address 114 Brooke Road.

The officer then contacted Supt. Hollands, head of the Elham Division, stationed at Seabrook Police Station in Folkestone who made his way to the scene and then passed the case to Edwin, and while awaiting his arrival made initial inquiries. Dr John R H Phillips, a local Hythe physician who carried out post mortems for the police, was also called. He arrived at the mortuary at 6.15pm and Edwin arrived while the post mortem was in progress.

The doctor informed him and the superintendent that putrefaction had already started but immediately discovered an incised, ragged edged wound four and a half inches long on the left side of the lower part of the neck. It was a deep wound extending through the tissues of the neck down to the back. In the lower edge of the wound he removed with tweezers two pieces of metal which he held up to the light but wasn't sure what they were. On the right side of the neck there was a slight wound, half an inch long and half an inch deep.

The body had, in his opinion, been in the water about four or five days and was newborn. Considerable force had been needed to inflict the wounds, but this depended a great deal on the weapon used. Examining closely he formed the conclusion that the pieces of metal were steel and had broken from some larger piece. His initial guess was that the wounds were caused prior to death because of the gaping and retraction of the tissues in the neck and the baby died through haemorrhaging and shock. He could not give an opinion on how long the child had lived after birth. He would need to do tests to establish whether the child had a separate existence and had breathed.

He turned to the two officers and commented, 'these cases are terrible, such a waste of life.'

'I have to agree and all too common. I'm not sure what we can do to stop it.'

'Sometimes during childbirth, women just go completely off their heads,' the doctor said shaking his head.

'So what's your next move Edwin and what can we do to help?' asked the superintendent.

Well the only clue we have is this damn address on the towel which I take it doesn't match any street locally?'

'No, not to my knowledge.'

'And I think we can agree that the mother must be local as on past experience these mothers do tend to abandon them close to home.'

'Again, agreed. I can't see anyone travelling all the way here from a distance just to place it in the canal in the middle of town.'

'So could you get your officers to canvas local doctors to see how many pregnant women they have seen who were about to give birth and who they remember might have acted strangely?'

'I'll get them on it straight away.'

An inquest was held two days later, and Dr Phillips stated he had completed an aeration test on the lungs, and he was satisfied that the child had breathed, but could not swear that the child had a separate existence. The verdict reached by the jury was that of wilful murder by some person or persons unknown.'

Sergeant Curtis was one of the officers given the delicate task of interviewing local doctors in search of the possible mother of the child. It was not any easy one as not all of the doctors were forthcoming at giving such private information, but after several days Edwin had narrowed it down to a local girl from the small village of Burmarsh a few miles from Hythe named Agnes Lydia Greenstreet.

*

Agnes Lydia Greenstreet was twenty-three years old and was born in 1880 in the market town of Ashford and lived with her parents John and Betsy and had two younger brothers John and Arthur. The family moved several times with her father seeking work and ended up in Aldington, a small village on the outskirts of Romney Marsh. Like many young unmarried girls there was little employment to be had in the bleak surroundings of the marsh and working in service was her only option. Many girls at the time would start their careers locally and then migrate to London in search of better prospects and a husband. She worked in several local houses including that of Mr Walton, a member of the Institute of Civil Engineers and lived in Hythe. She was in his service as a house parlour maid from spring 1900 to the end of the year and then worked as a housemaid for Mr Henry Cobay, an auctioneer and house furnishers at 40 High Street, Hythe.

At age seventeen Agnes had become involved with a local young man named Frederick Maycock, who worked as a groom and lived most of the time with his parents at 13 Rampart Road in Hythe not far from Agnes's parents. It proved to be a long-term relationship lasting five years and Agnes was more enamoured and faithful to the relationship than Fred. As the years past there were spells when they were apart with both of them working away from home. Agnes was of course expectant of marriage at some stage, but Fred was rather reticent in popping the question. Two years earlier the relationship had become more serious though and they began sleeping together whenever the opportunity arose. Finally, earlier the previous year Fred finally relented and proposed, and Agnes was ecstatic at being engaged. They decided to get married in September 1902 and she had spent weeks making her wedding dress and other clothing for her trousseau. But as September approached Fred postponed the wedding saying he might have to go to Isleworth in London to work for a while and suggested they wait until December when he was due to return and make it a Christmas wedding. Agnes had reluctantly agreed, but again as the time approached Fred cried off again and Agnes was obviously quite distraught and upset.

It was at this point that she began to feel sick and unwell and Fred kept commenting on how pale she looked and her lack of energy. Her mother also commented and Agnes herself had thoughts she might have the tell-tale signs of pregnancy but she cast these thoughts aside. Finally her mother succeeded in convincing her to visit Dr Clifford Hackney, the family doctor on 15 December and she explained the symptoms to him and he made a cursory examination of her chest and diagnosed anaemia as her ailments were symptomatic of that condition, including "shortness of breath, poverty of blood and irregularities in consequence," but initially he did not give her a full body examination even though anaemia was common in pregnant women. Three days later on the 18th he visited her at her parents' house and again gave her treatment for anaemia. Agnes went back to the doctor on several occasions and each time the Dr Hackney treated her for anaemia but no mention of pregnancy.

Agnes continued to put pressure on Fred by following him to London and finding a job as a parlourmaid with a Mr Munro in Stoke Newington. She was able to visit him on her days off. Fred obviously noticed that she was getting "stout" and looking weak and pale and asked her about it several times, but she kept telling him that she was O.K. After just four weeks Mr Munro asked her to leave because she felt so weak she did not perform her duties to his satisfaction.

Agnes was often short of breath, feeling light headed and generally poorly but didn't let on to Fred. When Mr Munro sacked her, she returned home, and her mother immediately called Dr. Hackney as she could see Agnes was unwell. He gave her a full examination at her mother's house on 29 January and was "suspicious" that she was pregnant and tried to tell her so without success and because of patient confidentiality didn't let on to her mother. Agnes clung on to the hope it was just anaemia, but if her mother was suspicious she didn't let on.

Finally on 4 March, at her parents' house, the doctor told her she was definitely pregnant and there was no doubt about it. Agnes cried her heart out knowing the implications of the announcement, particularly as Fred was so non-committal on getting married, but she couldn't fool herself any longer. She still kept quiet and said nothing to anyone still clinging to her lie of anaemia which ironically she did also have. Fred continued to badger her about her swelling belly until in the first week of April when she finally accepted the fact in her own mind and irritably said him, 'If there is anything you are the father of it.'

*

Agnes went in search of another job at the end of April fully aware of her predicament and answered an advertisement for a parlourmaid with a Mrs Emily Stone of 92 Bouverie Road West, Folkestone. Mrs Stone was impressed with her, and she started work there on the 2 May 1903. Agnes was bedevilled by stomach pains, and she continued to cling to the hope that it was still something to do with her anaemia. She complained occasionally of pain and all the other staff were aware of her so-called ailment and had a sneaking suspicion of what was really wrong. It eventually came to the notice of her employer who asked her if she had consulted a doctor, and she said she had been regularly examined for six weeks by a Dr Hackney in Hythe. Mrs Stone asked her what he thought was wrong with her and she told her anaemia. Agnes knew that Mrs Stone was regularly visited by a Doctor Lennox Wainright, and she asked if Mrs Stone could arrange for her to see him. This she did and Agnes went to his house on the 1 July. She explained her symptoms and he asked if she had seen another doctor. When she told him she had been under treatment with Dr. Hackney he asked what he had diagnosed. She told him anaemia and that she was too fat. He told her he couldn't examine her, but she must go back to her own doctor for a thorough examination.

Two days later Mrs Stone enquired what had happened at the doctor's and Agnes told her that, 'the doctor didn't say much to me as I had already consulted another doctor. He just gave me a slight examination and was going to give me something which would do me good but would make me very ill for a few days. He said I looked relatively "stout", but anaemia would account for it.'

After that Agnes went about her work as normal until the morning of July 9 when Mrs Stone could not find her anywhere downstairs, and the other staff said they hadn't seen her as wasn't doing her work. She sent her cook, Florence Dodd up to find her. Flo knocked on her bedroom door but got no answer, so she went in finding Agnes lying on her bed.

'Are you feeling alright, Aggie? You look proper queer.'

'I'm feeling really poorly Flo with stomach pains. I want to go home,' replied Agnes in an anguished voice.

'Mrs Stone is really worried about you. Do you want me to call her?'

'No don't do that. I'll be down soon.'

But the pains got worse and kept coming in waves, so she remained on the bed. When she didn't appear Flo was so worried she went back to check on her.'

'Come on Aggie you can't just lay here all day; you'll get the sack.'

'The pains are worse Flo. I'll be down soon. Promise.'

At about 1.50pm Mrs Stone and Flo went up to her again still worried but the door was locked so they spoke to her through the door now really concerned.

Flo called through the door, 'Don't worry I'm much better. I'm coming down.'

When she went downstairs Mrs Stone decided she should go home to her mother to be nursed. She ordered a cab for her to pick up her up at two o'clock.

'Mrs Stone says I can go with you to make sure she got there safely,' offered Flo.

'It's alright Flo, I can manage. I'll just pack a few things.'

Agnes disappeared upstairs again.

*

On Wednesday 9 July 1903 William Doggett was having a busy day. He was a taxi driver and lived at 15 Sheldon Street, Folkestone in Kent, a popular seaside resort. Being summer the town was thronged with holidaymakers enjoying the sunny weather. In the afternoon he was hailed to 92 Bouverie Road West. He stopped at the three-storey semidetached mansion, tied up his horse, and walked to the front door on the side of the house. He rang the bell and waited. It was opened by Flo and as he usually did he asked if there was any luggage to take. On being told no he went back to his cab to wait. After ten minutes or so he became agitated as there was no sign of his fare. As with all cab drivers time was money and he could ill afford to hang around.

Flo having answered the door went up to fetch Agnes, but the bedroom door was locked. She called but received no reply so she went and found Mrs Stone who went up to her room on the top floor and told her not to be silly and to come out quickly as the cab would not wait much longer. Agnes shouted back she would be down in ten minutes, but Mrs Stone could not understand what she was doing and was rather annoyed.

When she did come down carrying a parcel which Mrs Stone presumed was some of her belongings she could see that Agnes was very pale and frail and did not look well at all. She stood at the front door with Flo to wave her off and shouted after her 'I hope you will get better soon.' Flo went to Agnes's room and was shocked to see blood splattered across the floor where she had last seen Agnes standing. Blood was also on the washstand basin.

*

It was nearly twenty minutes before William spotted a good-looking young lady came down the path carrying a brown paper parcel under her arm. He helped her into the cab which was open to the air being a warm day. She asked for the roof to be closed which he thought strange but did so. He noticed that the lady was rather subdued and unwilling to pass the time of day so after a few attempts at conversation he gave up. She asked him to take her to the Swan Commercial Hotel at 67 Hythe High Street, another seaside resort some four miles west along the coast. William was more cheerful now as it was an out-of-town fare, and he set off at a trot. He kept a furtive eye on the lady as she didn't seem well and was acting strangely. As they entered Hythe the lady shouted to him to pull up outside the Bell public house about half a mile from Hythe High Street. She paid the six-shilling fare and walked towards the High Street. William opened the roof again and as he was doing it he noticed a clot of blood on the carpet which concerned him, but she had already passed from sight, so he turned the horse and headed back to Folkestone.

*

When Agnes got out of the cab she had made sure the driver wasn't looking and crossed the road and walked down Twiss Road exactly opposite the Bell Inn and headed towards the canal and sea front. When she got to the canal she crossed the bridge and then turned left along the tow path. She walked twenty yards and sat down on the bank with the parcel on her lap. There was no one else on the tow path and no river traffic. She sat there crying and moaning, communing with her dead baby and in a possessed state not knowing which way to turn. After a while she crouched and gently floated the parcel containing the baby on to the still water, turned and headed back to the high street and walked to the house of her boyfriend's mother, Elizabeth and Frederick Maycock, arriving at about quarter to four.

Elizabeth was alone and let her in noticing she was in quite a state. Agnes told her she had been ill, and her mistress had sent her home for a few day's rest. Elizabeth made her a cup of tea and tried to cheer her up but realised something was very wrong. Just before 6pm Agnes announced that she was going to see Fred, and Elizabeth seeing how exhausted and ill she looked, tried to dissuade her and begged her to stay and rest but she left. Fred was a groom and worked at 8 Douglas Avenue, Hythe, a few streets away and she found him at the stables where he was surprised to see her.

'Hello, what on earth are you doing here. You know they don't like visitors.'

'I had to see you.'

'Why, what is so urgent. You are looking very queer.'

'Oh, I'm alright.'

'Well you don't look it.'

'I haven't been very well, and my missus has sent me home for a few day's holiday, but I must go back on Monday. I will write and let you know.'

'How are you getting home?

'I will take cab, will you come with me?'

Fred said he couldn't get away for at least an hour but shouted after her, 'Mind you have a rest.'

She walked back to his parent's house and rested a while, and then hailed a cab and returned home to Burmash.

Mrs Stone had been so concerned about her that she went to her home the following Tuesday to see how she was. Agnes told her she was feeling better but had decided not to return to work and would come and collect her belongings later.

*

Edwin's investigations continued over the next few days and he was finally sure that he had found the mother. He had been cautious as he did not want to accuse the wrong woman of killing her baby. It was a delicate situation, but on the 17 July Edwin and Albert accompanied by the local constable made their way to a farm cottage in Burmarsh where she was allegedly staying with a family friend. Agnes was surprised they had found her and Edwin explained why they were there and began to interview her.

'Can you give me your full name and age,' he asked.

'Agnes Lydia Greenstreet and I am 23 years old,' she replied.

'Have long have you been staying here?'

'Since Thursday 9 July.'

'And where did you live previously to this?'

'At 92 Bouverie Road in Folkestone with Mrs Stone.'

'Did you also once live in service at 114 Brooke Road in London?'

'Yes I lived there.'

'And when did you leave?'

'I left last February.'

'The body of a child has been found in the canal at Hythe and I suspect you of being the mother. Am I correct in thinking that?'

'Really. I have no idea of what you are talking about.'

'An inquest has been held and a verdict of wilful murder has been returned by the jury against some person or persons unknown.'

'Good gracious you don't think I know anything about that do you?'

'I'm afraid we do. I don't want you to say anything else but whatever you do say will be used in evidence against you.'

'But I've told you, I know nothing about this,' wailed Agnes.

'I'm sorry, I must charge you on suspicion of having murdered your child and you must consider yourself in custody, and you will be conveyed to Seabrook Police Station.

'But I have never had a baby; I have been suffering from anaemia,' she shouted.

Edwin searched Agnes's room and her box of belongings but didn't find any baby clothes in preparation for birth anywhere in the room or elsewhere in the house. It seemed that Agnes had been in a state of mind where she had blanked out any acceptance that she was about to give birth. He felt sorry for her but realised this refusal made the killing of her baby seem premeditated.

When Agnes had calmed down he escorted her out of the cottage into a carriage and took her to Seabrook police Station where she was charged with murder.

*

Edwin liked to be thorough, he was well known in judicial circles for it, and his investigations had been extensive making sure he had an airtight case to go before the magistrates, particularly as Agnes had not admitted to the murder. He had interviewed Dr Hackney and Dr. Wainwright, along with Agnes's former employers and staff, spoken to her boyfriend Fred and his mother, the taxi driver and Mr Drury, the finder of the body. The label had taken him to London to visit the Star Steam Laundry Company in Hackney Downs where he had spoken to Ernest John Smith the manager. Edwin handed him the label and Mr Smith examined it and immediately confirmed it was one of theirs.

'Are you able to give us the name of the customer and full address?' asked Edwin.

'I'm sure it will be in the ledger if they are a regular,' he replied putting on his glasses and reaching for a heavy bound ledger.

He flipped through it and then said, 'Here we are. The customer is a Mr Munro, and his address is 114 Brooke Road Stoke Newington. It must be an old label as it written by one of my former employees named Spalding, but he left a couple of months previously, I'm afraid.'

'No matter we just wanted to confirm the address. You have been a great help.'

Edwin then caught a cab to Brooke Road where the house maid let him in and announced him.

'Sorry to disturb you, Mr Munro. I am Det. Sgt. Fowle of Kent County Constabulary.'

'You are a long way from home Sergeant. What on earth do you want from me?'

'I am looking for information about an Agnes Greenstreet who I believe once worked for you.'

'Oh poor Agnes, yes I remember her.'

'You say poor Agnes. Was there a problem.'

'Well it was only a fleeting employment. I took her on as a housemaid in January this year and she did come with references, but she was very discontented here, complaining of illness and weakness and quite sullen and distracted as though the weight of the world was on her.'

'Do you know why?'

'No. I tried asking her, but she wouldn't tell. I did not think it was beneficial to keep her so after a month I let her go.'

'I see. Do you know where she went?'

'I'm afraid not.'

'Do you have any other servants who might know more about her?'

'There's Mary. I'll call her.'

Mary Ann Wilson had been working for Munro from 17 December 1902.

'Did you have a chance to get to know Agnes during her short stay?'

'Not really. We shared a bedroom, but she wasn't much fun.'

'Why is that?'

'She was always complaining about being anaemic and suffering pains in her stomach. She seemed to think of nothing else.

'Did she see a doctor?'

'She said she'd been under a doctor for six weeks before coming to London. I told her she was pregnant. She had all the symptoms, but she wouldn't have it. Kept harping on about being anaemic and that's what the doctor had treated for.'

'Thank you, Mary.'

Edwin was happy he had enough to prosecute poor Agnes.

*

In total there were three magistrate hearings held and at the first on Saturday 18 July only sufficient evidence was offered to justify a remand which was granted until Tuesday 23rd. Although Edwin preferred to stay out of the limelight he was in the news again on the 25 July with a headline in the *Folkestone Express* announcing that:

> *The mystery surrounding the death of a newly born female child whose body was found in the Hythe canal last week has, through the efforts of Det. Sgt. Fowle, been solved.*

By the time the second hearing took place the news had spread throughout the district and aroused considerable interest. Long before 11am when the hearing was due to start the area outside the Sessions Hall police court in Bank Street was crowded with onlookers keen to catch a glimpse of Agnes who was described in the press as a "fine looking woman." She arrived at the Court in a cab and was hurried in. When the doors were thrown open to the public there was a great rush to gain admittance, but the public area was small, and many were disappointed.

When Agnes was placed in the dock she was charged with wilfully murdering a certain newly born female child and she sobbed uncontrollably while listening. Supt. Hollands stated that the case had now been placed in the hands of the treasury and he had been instructed to apply for a remand for a week to give them time to familiarise themselves with the case. This was granted, but Mr Drake, who had been engaged to represented Agnes, objected and pointed out that all the witnesses were present and surely it would be beneficial by taking the evidence of some of them that morning in order to lessen the case next time and save the poor girl extra distress. Eventually, however, after consultation with the magistrates clerk, Mr Drake consented to withdraw his application. The case was adjourned until the following Tuesday.

Outside a large crowd watched as the very weak Agnes was assisted into a cab by four constables who were there to regulate the crowd and taken by Edwin to Seabrook police station.

*

Agnes was back in court for the last hearing on Monday 27 July and was greeted by a large crowd numbering over two hundred eagerly anticipating her arrival. The courtroom was soon filled to capacity. The case should have commenced at 11am but the late arrival of the Canterbury train transporting her from the female prison in the town delayed matters.

They had congregated at the magistrate's entrance to get a good view of her as she stepped from the carriage, but Edwin and the superintendent had outwitted them by driving her by a back lane which caused great disappointment, but they behaved with decorum and there was no unseemly demonstration. Once the four magistrates had taken their seats the clerk nodded for the doors to be opened and a row of policemen stationed there by the Superintendent formed a barrier to guide them in, but only about half of those waiting gained entry.

Once the onlookers had settled and order was restored, Agnes was led in and there were audible expressions of sympathy and support. She wore a black frock, green jacket and white straw hat. She appeared to be in a dazed condition and sat at the side of the court between a wardress, and a well-dressed and dignified locally famous sixty-year-old lady named Mrs (Henry) Sarah Kingsley. She was well known in Hythe and nationally as an outspoken temperance advocate. She had been unanimously elected President of the Hythe & District United Temperance Council and was President of the Girls' Rescue Society which helped destitute and fallen young women. She supported many other societies and took her temperance work very seriously giving speeches all over the southeast and in London. Prior to moving to Sandgate near Hythe she had lived in Wimbledon, London which she described as a place with "an enormous amount of indifference and a great deal of sin." There she earnestly campaigned to close down drinking establishments and changes in licensing laws which incensed many men so much that she was often verbally attacked, and also upset the local press who referred to her as the Demon of Discord. In her voluntary capacity as a member of the Ladies Visiting Committee of the Elham Union Workhouse she often visited the women's and children's wards where she had a background of befriending young women particularly of the servant class who had passed through the workhouse system and needed help.

Mr F J Williamson, the Treasury solicitor prosecuted while Mr F Drake, a local solicitor who had been hired by Mrs Kingsley, defended. Mr Williamson gave a long and detailed account of the case and then called all the witnesses.

Agnes was given assistance to enter the barriers that acted as the dock by Mrs Kingsley who whispered support to her. Due to her pale and weary state she was accommodated with a chair. Agnes looked a pitiable sight and at first, she stared vacantly round the court and appeared to "acutely feel the gravity of her situation." In a clear and distinct voice the magistrates clerk, Mr G S Wilkes read over the charge to her and once or twice she gave way to weeping.

The prosecution put forward the facts of the case and then called a string of witnesses that Edwin had interviewed including Dr Clifford Hackney, Dr Lennox Wainright, Dr John Phillips, Albert Munro, George Drury, P.C. Wills, the Superintendent, Earnest Smith, Mary Wilson, Emily Stone, Elizabeth Maycock, Frederick Maycock and the last witness was Edwin.

It was about half-past three when Mr Drake rose and addressed the bench. He did not call any defence witnesses but proceeded to give an "eloquent and forcible" speech pointing out that the prosecution had utterly failed to prove the case against his client. He then re-examined Dr Hackney and took exception to his conduct in breaking patient confidentiality by telling the police of her condition but not informng her mother.

Mr Drake asked the doctor, 'To whom did you volunteer the statement that you attended this girl? Was it of your own initiative?'

'To the sergeant of police when he asked me if I had attended a girl who had recently been confined,' answered the doctor.

'And you gave Sgt. Curtis the whole information?'

'Yes, I gave him my visiting list and showed him the names.'

'Did you tell the sergeant you had attended this girl?'

'No. He mentioned the name first.'

'Did you then say you attended her?'

'Yes, but is that me volunteering the information?' the doctor asked Mr Drake pointedly.

'I don't wish to be hard or cruel in any way to you doctor, or treat you unprofessionally, but would you volunteer information to any old policeman who came along?'

'Yes, certainly.'

Then you don't consider that you are pledged to your patient's secrecy?'

'I don't consider so. In the interests of justice I consider that I was right in giving the information.'

'I believe you attended this girl at her mother's house?'

'I did.'

'Did you ever communicate anything to her mother as to her condition?'

'I did not.'

'I see.'

At this point the prosecutor asked the doctor, 'At the time you gave the information to the police, did you know that the child had been found murdered?'

'Yes, that a child had been murdered.'

He then berated Dr Lennox Wainwright for turning her away and finally gave Fred Maycock a grilling and asked:

'Were you going to get married to this girl in September?'

'Yes,' answered Mayock hesitantly.

'You were engaged to her, were you not?'

'Yes.'

'When was the wedding to take place?'

'Well, it was not settled,' replied Mayock nervously.

'Do you mean to say that it was not settled to take place last September?' asked Mr Drake firmly.

'Yes.'

'Did you know as a matter of fact that this poor girl had got the whole of her wedding clothes ready last September?'

'I don't know.'

'Are you at the present moment still engaged to be married to her?'

'I suppose.'

'I don't want your suppositions, sir. Answer yes or no. You refuse to answer, I suppose?'

'Yes.'

'I would say you have treated this poor girl rather abominably.'

Mr Drake then gave a forcible closing speech:

> I wish the testimony of Dr Hackney had not been given as I believe a medical man who has the confidence of his patients should under no circumstances betray that confidence. The doctor has said that that he had attended the girl at her mother's house, and it was his duty to inform her mother, and had he done so the girl would never have been brought to the court. I believe any jury of twelve competent men would ever bring in a verdict of "Guilty" from such a prosecution as this; even if the jury consisted of a thousand men, not one in that thousand would say that my client was guilty.

He then addressed the jury:

> First of all you must conclude that the child was born alive and on that hinges the whole case. The prosecution has not proven this or that it had a separate existence and in support I must call the evidence of Dr Phillips to your attention on whose evidence no jury could return a guilty

> verdict. I am prepared to meet any further prosecution with all the powers I have in my body and urge the Bench to say there is no case for the jury to dwell on. I urge this for this reason. The Assizes does not open for another three months and what the poor girl has already suffered nobody knows. What she wll suffer if the bench says that she must go back to prison I cannot venture to suggest. The keen remorse she would suffer during these three months would be too awful for a girl to bear. I ask that you can find the compassion to dismiss her and allow bail to allow her to go home where she could get the consolation and comfort which under the circumstances she was greatly in need of.

Listening attentively to these words Agnes completely broke down sobbing and crying bitterly. Mrs Kingsley put her arm round the girl's neck and endeavoured to comfort her. The magistrates then left the court to deliberate and by the time they returned she had regained her composure. She was told to stand, and the Chairman spoke to her:

> Agnes Greenstreet, the bench has given the case most serious consideration, and they have concluded that there is sufficient evidence in the case to warrant us in committing you to take your trial at the Maidstone Assizes.

Agnes gave no sign of emotion on hearing their decision but slumped slightly and when the clerk read the charge over to her again she turned to the public gallery and said in a firm and clear voice "I am not guilty." She was returned to Canterbury prison and as she stepped into a waiting cab the large crowd fell silent.

*

On Thursday 26 November Agnes appeared before Justice Lawrence on the charge of feloniously, wilfully and of her own malice aforethought killing and murdering a certain female child, lately before then born of her body and not then named at Hythe on the 9 July 1903. Mr H C Croft appeared for the prosecution and Mr Hohler defended.

Agnes, who had been incarcerated in the austere Maidstone prison nearly four months, was forced to patiently wait all day to discover her fate as it was 5pm before she entered the dock at the Maidstone Assize court. Remarkably she had according to the *Folkestone Express* a "cheerful countenance and gazed in wonderment around the court" while the jury were sworn in. A true bill was returned by the grand jury and in reply to the formal accusation she said in a clear voice "Not Guilty." It was probably evident that during the day there had been some plea-bargaining taking place of which she was aware.

Before proceedings started there was a conference between the two counsels and to many people's surprise Mr Croft consented to reduce the capital charge to the lesser concealment of birth to which Agnes immediately pleaded "Guilty."

Under the circumstances, none of the witnesses who appeared at the police court were called, but Mr Hohler, addressed the judge remarking that it was a particularly sad case. The woman had borne an excellent character, and she was to be pitied. It was one of those unfortunate cases in which a man has seduced her at a time when he promised to marry her. His name was 23-year-old Maycock and twice he fixed a date for the wedding and twice postponed it. So mean was his character that when before the magistrates court, the question was put to him as to whether he was engaged to her, he refused to say. Maycock left her to her fate.

One thing strongly in the woman's favour was that on July 1 she went to see Doctor Wainwright of Folkestone about her condition and told him that she had been suffering from anaemia and stout figure. The doctor asked if she had been attended by any other medical man and the prisoner said yes, a Doctor Hackney in Hythe. Whereupon he replied that he had no advice to give her. Naturally, the woman did not believe that she was pregnant, and she even asked Maycock her boyfriend, who assured her that she was not. Eventually she suffered from pains and delivered a child whose body was found in the canal at Hythe. Concluding Mr Hohler mentioned that two friends in Hythe were quite willing to look after her and she was prepared to go with them.

Mr Walton was then called to give evidence as to her character. He stated that he was a member of the Institute of Civil Engineers and lived in Hythe. He knew the prisoner well and she had been in his service as a house parlour maid from the spring 1900 to the end of the year. During that time he had every reason to suppose from her conduct that she was a modest, well-behaved woman. He felt sure that if it had not been for the misconduct of Maycock nothing would have happened which would have placed her in the unhappy position she stood in today. When in service with him he knew she was engaged to the young fellow Maycock, and he certainly believed her to be thoroughly well behaved and of a good disposition. He hoped his Lordship would give her an opportunity for redeeming her character.

Mr Hohler also advised the judge that Mrs Stone another employer could also give evidence to her character, but the judge said it was not necessary and she was not called. The judge, in addressing the prisoner, said:

> Agnes Greenstreet you have pleaded guilty to concealing the birth of this child, and no doubt you did. I am afraid you used considerable art in doing so. It is quite true, as Counsel has said, that it was in your favour as far as believing you were pregnant that you did apply to a second doctor at Folkestone. That doctor heard you had been to another doctor at Hythe and therefore refused to give you advice. That, certainly, is evidence in your favour in respect of your knowledge, whether you are pregnant or not; but, as I have said before, I am afraid you used considerable art in concealing the fact that you had given birth to a child. There are other cases which I don't care to mention that makes yours a serious one, but I hope this will be a warning to you. The sentence that I pass upon you is that you be kept in hard labour for eight calendar months.

According to one reporter, "there was considerable surprise in the court and an audible gasp and hardly had the last sentence fallen from the judge's lips when Agnes visibly crumpled in the dock in shock." She was described as in a pitiable spectacle as with a look of horror on hearing the sentence she froze until the warder touched her arm. She jumped and dropped a parcel she was holding containing some of her things in anticipation of being released. She valiantly tried to clutch the dock rail before dramatically collapsing into the arms of the warder. She was carried below amidst an excited uproar in the Court. Seconds later the warder reappeared up in the dock and grabbed the vessel of water kept there. It was obvious she had not been expecting such a severe sentencing. The case only occupied about eight minutes.

Agnes served her sentence stoically and when released returned to service work gaining a position in 1905 as a live in parlour maid for an elderly widow, Mrs Dure at 59 Marlborough Mansions in Hampstead, London and managed to continue a normal life. She met William Fiveash, a house painter, and married him in 1910 moving into a house in 14 Alexandra Road Hampstead. They had a son named William in 1911 and she continued living there until her death in 1951.

7

An Audacious Burglary at Bourne Grange (1908)

It was a very dark night, and the fog was getting thicker, much to their satisfaction. If fact it was proving a better night for the two men crouched in the shadows of a hedge than they could have wished for. They had travelled down from London to Tonbridge by train late that afternoon and had been to an ale house to help steady their nerves. Not that they needed to as they were relatively confident about their criminal undertaking. At about 8pm they made their way to Bourne Grange three miles outside Tonbridge, a mansion and estate belonging to Colonel James Menzies Clayhills, local justice of the peace and a prominent figure in the area, known for being one of the few survivors of the "thin red line" in the Crimean war battle of Balaclava. One of the men was carrying a short stout cudgel to break into the house but along the way they became worried it might not be sufficient, so they looked round for another implement they could use. As they walked across the estate they came across a damaged iron railing fence and managed to wrench one of the railings from the it. This could be very useful one of them said, waving it around and his companion smiled.

They were aware that the owners were not in residence and had taken all the household staff with them to their London residence at 66 Chester Square in Belgravia near Victoria railway station. They had made sure the family were still there before they left London. Both men were in fact very familiar with both the grounds and interior of the house, and the habits of the residents. They peered across the large expanse of lawn as best they could towards the large mansion and watched as the last light at the front was extinguished by Mr Leaney the gardener who was acting as caretaker.

He had been working for the Colonel for three years and it was a regular occurrence. It was his duty to make sure all the house was locked tight, and the only entrance used was at the back so at 10pm every evening he would walk all round the building and outhouses making sure everywhere was secure before locking and bolting the back door and going upstairs to sleep with his wife. That evening he had no idea all his movements were being watched by a pair of eyes in one of the garden borders. The two men then cautiously moved to the rear of the house where they knew the servants quarters were and watched as the caretaker and his wife put out their lamp. They silently moved back to the front and crossed the lawn quickly to the window of what they knew was the dining room.

One of the men whose name was Davite swiftly hit a small pane in the dining room window with the cudgel smashing it and causing more noise than they anticipated. The other man, Julian, swore and slapped Davite for hitting the window too hard. Both men crouched, their hearts beating as they prepared to run. They waited a few minutes while Davite attempted to locate the source of the blood that was trickling from his hand which had obviously been cut while breaking the window. Once convinced that the gardener had not heard them, they unlatched and opened the window, forced the wooden shutters and climbed in being careful not to disturb any furniture or ornaments.

Once inside they lit a candle and made straight for three oil paintings hanging on the walls. They quietly and methodically cut the pictures from the frames and rolled the canvases up.

'Now for the drawing room' one Julian whispered.

'Right behind you, Jules. This is proving easier than I thought.'

'Don't count your chickens yet,' warned Davite.

The two men edged to the door and John grabbed the doorknob, but the door was locked.

'What's up?'

'The blimming door is locked.'

'Who for chrissakes, locks an internal door?'

'The blimming gardener, that's who.'

Julian wedged the iron bar in the door in an attempt to force it open.

'Don't do that, you'll make too much noise,' whispered Davite.

'So what now?' asked Julian.

'We'll have to go out the window and round to the drawing room window and break that.'

'Risky ain't it?'

'I'm not leaving here without gold and silver.'

They carefully climbed out and crept along the front of the mansion and broke another window and pulled back the latch. They climbed into the drawing room and began rifling the drawers and filling two sacks they had brought with them.

Julian grabbed three valuable empire clocks and some gold and silver heirlooms.

'Don't forget the fire screen Davite.'

Davite got the knife out and cut the embroidery from the screen rolling it up and putting it with the paintings while Davite started searching the sideboard drawers.

'They didn't take the silver plate with them.' He started to remove the items.

'Leave them, we'll never be able to carry it all.'

'Course we will.'

'Not if we take the two vases.'

'But they're worse to carry.'

'Yeh, but easier to get rid of.'

Davite lifted the vases from the mantlepiece and added them to their stash.

'Let's get out of here.'

Davite got out of the window first and then handed Julian the bags. They furtively crossed the lawn where Davite dropped the cudgel and didn't stop to pick it up. They disappeared back into the fog and started walking back to Tonbridge.

*

Next morning Leaney was up early and with no master or other staff to order him about, he and his wife had a leisurely breakfast. It was 7.30am before he was walking round the house and as he came level with the dining room window he was stunned to see it open as were the wooden inner shutters. He looked round perplexed and slightly anxious. He saw something lying in the middle of the lawn and walked over and found a heavy cudgel like stick. He rushed into the house and ran from room to room finding the dining and drawing room ransacked and realised the house had been burgled. He knew better than to touch anything and told his shocked wife, then headed off to contact the police.

*

The local Tonbridge police on receiving the report were thrown into a bit of a panic realising the seriousness and possible repercussions with the Colonel being such an important, not to mention rich local figure and worse still a justice of the peace. The station sergeant immediately contacted Superintendent Robert Styles, the Divisional commander who was based at the station and who soon called the local detective on the force and sent him along with several constables to the grange.

Detective Everett arrived first, rather excited at the prospect of investigating this crime as he could imagine it would be highly reported and a feather in his cap if he manged the solve the case and get the culprits. He was met by a distressed Mr Leaney who led him to the centre of the lawn and the cudgel lying there.

'You haven't touched it?' Everett asked the gardener.

'No sir, I knew better than do that.'

'Good man.'

'They must have dropped it in their hurry to get away.'

'I think you're right.'

Everett crouched and looked at it closely and noticed what looked like blood on it.'

'He must have cut himself.'

'On the broken glass, yes,' said Mr Leaney, 'I'll show you the broken window.'

Everett realised that the County detectives would soon arrive and that his time was limited to make initial inquiries in order to impress them. He was rather piqued that he couldn't be trusted to lead the investigation.

At the dining room window he sidestepped the ground below and leaned across to take a close look at the broken plate glass window and was surprised at its quarter inch thickness which would have taken quite a blow to shatter. He spotted bloodstains on the glass and the blind inside which was drawn down. There were footprints underneath the window in the flowerbed soil and distinct footprint depressions of two men leading to the window across the lawn. The footprints below the window did not show any tread making him believe the boots were covered in cloth of some type or stockings. He went through the front door into the hallway and Mr Leaney showed him the damaged dining room door.

'Was this locked?'

'Yes sir, I always lock the interior doors as well.'

Everett examined the door from the room to the hall which showed damage where they had tried to open it.

Meanwhile, realising the importance and possible complexity of the case, Supt. Styles immediately called in Edwin and his detectives from Maidstone and sent a telegram to the London home of the Colonel to inform him of the break in. Edwin received the message at 11am and immediately caught a train to Tonbridge where he was met by the superintendent and taken to the mansion. They were met by Everret and after pleasantries he showed his two senior officers the cudgel, window, footprints and the ransacked rooms.

'You have been busy Detective,' Edwin told him, 'A good report.'

'Thank you ,sir.'

At that moment a constable who had been searching the grounds came up with the iron bar from the fence which had also been discarded. Edwin examined it along with the cudgel and both had white marks and putty which corresponded with the colour of the door and windows. Edwin stared at the outlines of the paintings in the faded wallpaper and looked at the discarded frames.

'Whoever did this knew what they were doing and what to take.'

'Do we know what is missing?'

'Not yet.'

'Definitely the two paintings. Any idea what they were. Were they worth a lot?'

The superintendent said, 'I doubt it as I have been in the room several times and I know one of the pictures was of the Colonel dressed in his uniform of the 7th Royal Fusiliers standing by his white charger with his black retriever dog at his feet. And if I remember right there was one of some boats in a harbour. I don't think they were worth much.'

'So our thief probably was not expert then. I am not getting the impression that they were professional thieves.'

'Do you reckon it was one man or a gang?'

'Hard to say, but I reckon at least two as they had a lot to carry off.'

'I should think they were probably not local and have legged it back to London by train, don't you?'

'I agree' said the superintendent, 'I don't think any local villain would be audacious enough to rob the Colonel, but it must have been someone with local knowledge who was aware of the valuables here.'

'Well, I would say that any old house and estate was worth a pillage, but I take your point.'

'Working on a theory they were from London or out of town I think our first port of call should be the railway station.'

At Tonbridge railway station they spoke to James Higgins the porter and asked if he had seen any men looking or acting suspiciously the previous evening or that morning.

'Funny you should ask but at about 6am this morning when I arrived for work and went into the booking office I happened to see two unkempt men looking out of the window. They were on the seat on the left of the booking office and looked as though they had slept rough. They were struggling to handle two parcels, and I offered to help but they brushed me away. One was in the form of a roll securely fastened with what looked like a curtain sash cord which seemed a bit strange.'

'Did you notice anything else?' asked Edwin.

'You know how your eyes kind of get attracted to something out of place, well, I noticed that their boots were clean, but their trousers were very muddy. Didn't kind of match up if you know what I mean. Why clean your shoes but wear muddy trousers.'

'Would you recognise them again?'

'Think so, particularly the one who had long black hair.'

'Anything else?'

'I overheard them talking and one definitely spoke with a foreign accent.'

'Did you see them leave?'

'Yeh, they got on the 7.14am train to Charing Cross using the return halves of tickets issued from there.'

'That's got to be them,' said Edwin to Det. Everrett.

'What next?'

'Time to involve our colleagues in London, I reckon.' Edwin sent a telegram to Scotland Yard with descriptions of the men, the vases and paintings.

*

Completely by chance that Saturday evening Det. Inspector Reynold Hawkins of Vine Street Metropolitan Police was wandering along Wardour Street, Soho, a hotspot for vice, and known for its dodgy antique and pawn shops and general villainy. He was an old hand who had the usual copper's nose for searching out suspicious behaviour. The Inspector was completely unaware of the burglary in Tonbridge but spotted two dishevelled men peering into antique shop windows each holding in full view a much-decorated vase. They did not seem to fit the description of owners of such valuable looking items.

'Hello, what have we got here then,' he thought to himself. Being in plain clothes he did not look out of place leaning against a post the other side of the street while he watched as one of the men went into number 141 with a vase only to reappear still clutching it a few minutes later. The two men walked further up the street and the Inspector tailed them. The same man then went into number 147, and then into 138 another antique shop with the same result. The Inspector crossed the road as the man came out and accosted them.

'Stop there you two. What are you up to?'

'Who are you?'

'I'm a police officer who d'you think,' said the Inspector brandishing his warrant card.

'What's the problem officer.'

'Where did you get these vases from?'

'Well it's a long story actually.'

'Well I've got plenty of time,' smiled the Inspector.

'It's like this officer. A man named Gregory gave them to us this morning in Bloomsbury High Street and asked us to sell them for him.'

'And you expect me to believe that. Where does he live?'

'At 24 High Street. Honest.'

'Is he a friend of yours?'

'Not really.'

'So you are telling me that a complete stranger accosts you with two expensive vases in the street and he trusts you to sell them for him and bring him the money?'

'That's right. We are to meet him somewhere in the Strand tonight. I don't know which part.'

'What kind of mug do you think I am. That's so stupid, it's almost believable. So you don't know which part, eh?' the Inspector asked sarcastically.

'No.'

'That's enough of this nonsense. I believe them to be stolen property, so I am detaining you until we can look into it. You'll have to accompany me to Vine Street police station.'

As luck would have it, back at the station the inspector discovered that a report had come in from Edwin about the burglary mentioning two vases and he immediately telegraphed him.

*

Edwin and Everett caught a later train and went to New Scotland Yard with some broken glass fragments and the stick to have finger print analysis. While he was there a message came through for him diverted from Tonbridge.

'Well. I'll be blowed,' exclaimed Edwin to Everett, 'two men have been detained at Vine Street police station in possession of two vases trying to pawn them in Soho.'

'You're kidding.'

'No, a detective spotted them not realising they were wanted by us at the time. How lucky for us. This will please the Colonel.'

'Those guys are pretty hapless.'

'I totally agree. I think they should find another occupation after this. I can't wait to meet them.'

At Vine Street Edwin was shown the vases and told Everett to take a cab over to 66 Chester Square to inform the Colonel of the good news and fetch someone to identify the vases. The Colonel turned up with Mary Pearson his cook cum house keeper, who helped identify them. He confirmed they were his and was congratulatory to Edwin and the other officers for their quick arrest.

*

Inspector Hawkins took Edwin to the cells and introduced him to the two forlorn looking men.

'May I introduce you to Julian Mahe aged 27, a former valet at the Grange now residing at 39 Dean Street, Soho and who left on the 14 May and this gentleman is Davite Adolphe, 19, waiter of 59 Kinnerton Street, Sloane Square who left on the 10 May.'

'We guessed the burglary was by someone who knew the house. Have you two got anything to say?' asked Edwin.

'I was never at the house. I stopped in Tonbridge waiting for Gregory and his friend to come back from the house and he gave me two vases, one for each of us to bring back to London and told us if we could sell them he would give us half the money. He said I will meet you in the Strand at half past five in the evening. We did not see him as we had been taken by the police.'

'That's a slightly different story than you told me earlier. What happened to Bloomsbury High Street?'

'And what about you, Mr Adolphe or whatever your name is?'

'I have nothing to say. It's only the same as he said.'

They were left in the cells, but an hour later they asked to see Edwin. They were brought up to an interview room and Edwin asked if they wanted to make a statement in writing. They replied that their writing was not good so could he do it for them. In it they still persisted that the mythical Gregory was behind it all and had asked Mahe to store the stolen items at his house in his locked storage box. He did not want to in case he got the blame for the burglary. He gave his address in Kinnerton Street and handed Edwin some keys.

Edwin, the Inspector and other local constables rushed to Kinnerton Street in Belgravia, a street and area occupied by servants, tradesmen and horse stabling who serviced their rich neighbours. They found Mahe's box and opened it with the key and found two clocks, two rugs, two plaques and art work in it. They searched the rest of property and found in a chest of drawers three pictures wrapped in a tablecloth with a piece of tapestry.

The two men appeared at Marlborough Street court on Monday morning charged with unlawful possession of the vases, but due to the fact that they were wanted for burglary in Kent, were transferred by the Court to the custody of Edwin who immediately arrested them on the charge. Edwin and Everrett escorted the prisoners in handcuffs by train to Tonbridge police station. In the train Edwin noticed a cut on Davite's hand and asked, 'how did you cut your hand?'

'I have no cut.'

'Show me your hand.' Edwin examined Adolphe's second finger on his right hand and found a recent cut. 'Looks like a cut to me.'

'I cut it on a nail in my pocket.'

'Really'

On Tuesday the two appeared at Tonbridge Magistrates court presided over by JG Talbot, MP and a full bench of justices, all friends and colleagues of the Colonel. They were charged with burglariously breaking and entering the dwelling house known as Bourne Grange, Hadlow, between the hours of 9pm and 6am on January 24th. and 25th. and stealing: "The Proposal" by F H Barnable of a lady wearing an indoor gown and holding a letter in her hand, a portrait of the Colonel dressed in his uniform of the 7th Royal fusiliers in 1864 standing by his white charger with his black retriever dog at his feet, also a painting of the entrance to Portsmouth harbour, two drawing room clocks and a hand painted fire screen valued at £200 and of course two large Japanese Kaga vases, the property of Colonel James Menzies Clayhills

In an interview for the *St Jame's Gazette* the Colonel commented that the "value of the stolen items was purely their personal value. Possibly the recent thefts of valuable pictures led the thieves to suppose that the canvasses they cut out might prove valuable." Both were remanded until Thursday 30th. The hearing was resumed on Thursday and Mrs Pearson, the Bourne Grange cook, with looks to kill glared at the two prisoners and described how she identified all the stolen items. The Colonel stated he was the owner of Bourne Grange which he used as a summer home and confirmed that the two men had been in his employ.

The Chairman said it was very satisfactory that the property was recovered and highly commended Edwin and the police for their energy, intelligence and zeal that they displayed throughout the case. They were committed for trial at the next Maidstone Assizes where they received 12 months hard labour.

8

Mysterious Disappearance of Pheobe Penniall (1905)

Phoebe Rebecca Penniall was the 32-year-old daughter of Daniel and Bridget. She had five siblings: three brothers and two sisters. Her father was a waterman bargeman working for the Thames Conservancy, and they lived in the poverty-stricken area of Greenwich at number 56 Thames Street, just set back from the waterside. Phoebe had moved to 17 Circus Street some half mile away near the park where she worked as a photographers assistant along with her sister Sarah. They were a highly religious family and Phoebe began training as a district visitor of the poor and a bible woman working for the West Greenwich Ragged School during the week and teaching at the Sunday bible school. Ragged Schools were charitable institutions which offered a haven for the poorest children excluded from education due to their behaviour and appearance. They provided free education in the form of basic reading, arithmetic and Bible reading. The children were also provided with food and clothing. The Ragged schools played an important part in the social and educational reform of the time, helping to lay the groundwork for the modern concept of free public education.

Phoebe loved helping the children and their families and when undertaking caring work in the community she dressed in a nun's uniform. She was adored and welcomed by the needy of the area and was highly respected by all who knew her. She was a good-looking woman; slim with fair hair, blue eyes, sharp features and petite at only 5ft 2 inches tall. People were always commenting that she looked younger than her age and was a genteel looking woman. She was a spinster and her sister Sarah had married years before but she had failed to find her soul mate.

But her life was to be turned upside down when she fell head over heels in love with a rich handsome married man she called Ted who frequented and supported the school. He was beguiled and charmed by her looks and manner and began to take an interest in her. Phoebe who was somewhat naïve in the matters of love quickly became besotted by his attention and a romance soon blossomed between them despite the fact that he was married. They became devoted to each other and she soon found herself living a double life, secretly meeting up with him and not telling her family.

Almost a year after her liaison began, and much to her horror, she realised she was pregnant, and the ramifications of this event were not lost on her. She had the reputation of being a virtuous lady from an equally religious family and this would destroy all her good work in the community. Having an illegitimate child often led to tragic outcomes for both the mothers and their newborns. She believed her family would support her but her status in the community would be destroyed, and she did not feel she could face the accusations. She discussed the situation with Ted and together they made the decision not to tell anybody, but they realised it was impossible to keep her condition secret for more than a few months.

By February her pregnancy was increasingly apparent, and she was anxious about the embarrassment she would cause to her family. Ted was extremely sympathetic to her predicament as it would also adversely impact him greatly being a well-known, successful and respected married businessman. He suggested that she might consider moving away completely from the area and cut ties with her family until after the baby was born and hopefully they could work something out, but neither of them had a plan which would allow her to continue her old life again. Divorce and marriage was not a consideration Ted could envisage at this stage. They realised desperate measures were required so he suggested looking for a position somewhere as a nurse, companion or nanny until he could organise something more permanent and they scanned the newspaper columns.

Eventually they came across an advertisement for a nurse companion to a fruit farmer's wife on a farm outside a village named Mereworth in Kent, midway between Maidstone and Sevenoaks. The farm was owned by Mr and Mrs Richards and was pleasantly situated among fruit orchards and rolling countryside. The couple had a young son and Mrs Richards was partially invalided and required help round the house and in dressing. As they travelled by train for an interview, Ted in a tender moment, made a mock proposal to her and gave her a ring to wear so that everyone would presume they were married. At the interview Phoebe and Mrs Richards immediately hit it off and the job was hers.

At the end of February she gave a tearful farewell to her parents and five siblings who were mystified and confused about her departure and tried to persuade her not to go, but she was adamant and they could not prevent her. It was the last time any of them they saw her, but initially they received regular letters in which she convinced them that she had settled in well. She wrote of short rambles in the countryside with her employer and son and how she was thoroughly enjoying the clean air and peace and quiet after the ugliness and dank polluted atmosphere of London.

But her parents began to get worried as they had no address for her and Phoebe insisted they sent letters as Poste Restante to Sevenoaks post office. Her refusal to divulge her address increasingly concerned and worried her parents who became suspicious thinking something was amiss or she was being kept against her will. When her mother pressured her and suggested they came for a visit she stopped writing but instead only communicated through her married sister, Mrs Billinghurst. Her family remained perplexed that they had been cut off.

On 11 August, a bizarre and mysterious series of events took place. Mrs Billingshurst received a letter supposedly from Phoebe stating she was very ill suffering from sunstroke. This obviously really worried her and she passed on the news to her parents. Soon after another postcard arrived saying she was "Feeling better, home again soon" and suggested she should visit her. She was strangely asked to the nearest station which was Wateringbury, the popular boating resort on River Medway, where a trap would be waiting outside to take her to a house named Yotes Place near Mereworth. But she could not make the day stipulated but asked to come the day before. She received a reply stating she could go that day but couldn't be picked up and would have to make her own way accompanied by a map marked with Yotes Place.

She accordingly went and tramped all-round the countryside for hours asking people if they had heard of the place but could find no trace of the house named in the letter or the people whose name her sister had given. She returned to London and gave the news to her parents who were distraught and insisted they would all return the next day to search. They were now beginning to believe the worst. On the following day, Phoebe's brother, mother, sister and her husband went down to Sevenoaks by train, hired transport and scoured the district with the hope of finding some news of Phoebe while her brother took a bicycle with him on the train and explored the countryside. They drove for about four hours, but without success.

The whole Pennial family was now convinced that something was very wrong and immediately reported Phoebe missing, possibly in Kent, to Scotland Yard who passed the details to the Kent County Constabulary to try and discover if Phoebe was alive or dead and what had happened to her.

*

Edwin was sitting in his office at Wrens Court when the missing woman report landed on his desk. He leaned back in his chair and quickly read it, 'Strange one this,' he mumbled to himself.

'Did you say something sarge?' asked Detective Constable Tom Luck as he walked passed the doorway.

'Looks like we have a strange case to investigate.'

Tom appeared back in the doorway. 'Strange how?' he asked.

'Young lady from what appears to be a very pious family in London seems to have disappeared and was last heard of near Sevenoaks. Her parents say it's out of character and her father believes she is still alive and being held against her will in some sinister way.'

'Seems a bit far-fetched about her being held hostage,' agreed Tom.

'Apparently she is a genteel pious lady who has devoted her life to preaching the gospel and helping the poor, particularly children. To all intents she was happy at home, then suddenly informed them she was taking up a job as a nurse companion on a farm but wouldn't divulge where.'

'That is odd. Sounds like she was running away from someone or something. When was this?'

'Back at the beginning of March.'

'So why take so long to report her missing?'

'Evidently she remained in contact with them for a while and they would send letters to the Sevenoaks post office for collection and she would answer, but they have heard nothing for a while. The Yard have asked us to see if we can track her down. They have sent a photograph, look,' said Edwin passing it to Tom.

'Wow, she is a looker,' said Tom admiringly as he studied the slim, fair-haired woman.

'Which may be her problem,' stated Edwin.

'So what do we think?'

'Methinks a visit to Sevenoaks post office is called for.'

*

Edwin and Tom made their way to Sevenoaks post office on St Johns Hill and introduced themselves to the postmaster.

'What can I do for you sirs?' he genially asked.

'Look at this photograph if you would. Do you recognise her?' asked Edwin.

The postmaster looked down his glasses and scrutinised the picture for a minute, 'Pretty girl I must say and yes I do. I remember her well because she came in here regularly to collect her correspondence. She strangely always opened them and then went over to the counter there and wrote replies and posted them before leaving.'

'Did she seem alright. Not worried or upset?'

'I can't say she did. Always had a smile and said thank you.'

'The letters never had an address on?' Edwin asked hopefully.

'Sorry no. they were just marked "to be collected."

'Have you any idea where she was living?'

'We did have the odd chat and I got the impression she was working on a farm somewhere near Wrotham.'

'When was the last time you saw her?'

'Last time must have been early May.'

'A while back then. And the letters stopped?'

'No. It was funny though because a man started coming in to collect them and he told me he was her brother. Soon after that the letters stopped coming altogether.'

'A man you say. Could you describe him?'

'From what I can remember he was well spoken and finely dressed. Obviously a gentleman. He was tall, quite thin and had a ginger pencil moustache if that helps.'

The two officers left the post office and Edwin turned to Tom.

'The plot thickens, eh Tom?'

'What next sarge?'

'Well I knew it was going to be too much to ask getting an address. Nothing is easy so we'll have to do it the hard way. First we'll go to Sevenoaks police station and have a word with Superintendent Hoare as it's his area and asked him to get his men on making local enquiries throughout the district to see if anyone has seen her. Then I want you to check out all the doctors and cottage hospitals in the area to see if they have treated her and I'll check out the Registrar to see if her death has been registered.'

'Do you think she is dead?'

'I'm not sure what to make of it all at the moment, but I think she may be.'

*

It wasn't long before the farm was traced when a local bobby recognised seeing Phoebe when on his patrols. Edwin and Tom made their way to the farm and interviewed the owners, Mr and Mrs Richards. They sat down in the cosy farmhouse kitchen with mugs of strong tea and spoke to Mrs Richards.

'We are trying to piece together the movements of Miss Penniall after she left London as her family have reported her missing.'

'Well I never. We had no idea. Of course knew her as Mrs Stanley and she told us she was recently married.'

'So she called herself Stanley. That is very helpful as we didn't know that.'

'Why missing when she was here all the time?' asked a bemused Mrs Richards.

'She had refused to give her address to her family and then stopped writing and obviously became quite concerned. Did you notice anything suspicious about her behaviour?'

'Well no. She stayed with us for two months and we got on like a house on fire. She was a pleasant young woman, a good carer and adored our son. We had no complaints and were sorry to see her leave.'

'What about the man she was with?'

'You mean her husband Ted. He was a real gentleman and apparently a very busy man in the city and only came down to see her for a day or an afternoon every week whenever he could get away from work.'

'I'm afraid Mrs Richards that they were not married,' Edwin informed her.

'Not married, well I never,' she said again. 'But she had a ring and they acted like a married couple. They were very loving and she was very depressed every time he went back. They would walk together enjoying the spring flowers and blossom or occasionally go for a tram ride in Maidstone. Most weeks on her day off we gave her a lift to Borough Green Station and she would get a train to Sevenoaks to shop and attend to things,'

'Did you think it was strange that he rarely visited.'

'I'm not sure I thought it strange but we felt sorry for her being parted from him most of the time but realised she wasn't that well and rather fragile and could understand her wanting to be away from the horrible city. I remember her saying that they were happy days for her living in such beautiful countryside after the ugliness of London. Everything was done by the gentleman for her happiness and comfort, and of course, I did not pry into their private business.'

'You knew she was pregnant?'

'We guessed particularly when she told us she must leave as she couldn't cope with the work.'

'Did she tell you where she was going.'

'She said Ted had placed an advertisement in the *Kent Messenger,* asking for a bed sitting room for her for two months and they soon found a room in Maidstone, but I don't know the exact address. I hate to think that anything awful has happened to her as we she greatly endeared herself to us.'

'So do I,' agreed Edwin.

*

Having made inquiries at the newspaper office Edwin discovered that two spinster sisters named Richardson had answered the advert. They lived at 6 Albany Street, a quiet cul-de-sac just north of Maidstone town centre, where they let out rooms on the upper floor of their terraced house and apparently Phoebe had been living there for several months. He quickly visited them to discover more and sat in their parlour over tea to interview them.

'Can you tell us, in as much detail as possible, how Phoebe came to be lodging with you?'

'We run a respectable house sergeant and when our tenant had just vacated, we noticed an advert in the local paper from a lady requiring a bed sitting room for two months, so we made contact. It seemed heaven sent for us as we prefer to rent rooms to women as they are less trouble. We wrote a letter offering the accommodation subject to interview and received an answer from a man who suggested that he viewed the accommodation first as he wanted it for his wife who wasn't well and wished some country air for a few months.'

'When was this?'

'At the end of April.'

'What was his name?'

'He said his name was Mr Stanley.'

'Could you describe him?'

'He was an obviously a gentleman well educated, refined and smartly dressed in his thirties perhaps quite tall and thin with a small moustache.'

'What did he say to you?'

'He arrived on Thursday 27 April and was very charming but we were shocked when he explained that his wife was pregnant and expected to be confined in July, but her health was poor and he wished her to get some country air away from the city. We were very doubtful and a little concerned about taking her in as we didn't really want to get involved with her having a child here but he used his charm to convince us that he would arrange for a nurse and doctor to be on call and pay all expenses when the time came and we decided to trust him.'

'When did you meet his wife?'

'She came alone two days later on the Saturday by taxi with a trunk, a cardboard Tate and Lyle sugar box and a basket and was delighted with the room. We thought it strange her husband didn't help her. She was very pretty and amiable and we were immediately taken with her. She explained she was newly married and seemed in love. It was very sweet.'

'And you believed the story?' asked Edwin.

'The lady had a wedding ring on and also had two other rings. I had no inkling that they were unmarried. She was well dressed and wearing a brooch and other jewellery. They always acted very loving just as newlyweds should act. She called him Ted.'

'When did you see Mr Stanley next?'

'He came down by train from London and visited every Tuesday, Thursday or Friday afternoon. He only stayed for a few hours and had tea with her and then he was off. She would accompany him to the station to see him off and always returned looking glum.'

'Didn't you find that odd and ask why?' asked Edwin.

'Well I thought it inappropriate for me to ask and I just guessed they may have had a secret marriage.'

'Did she have any other callers?'

'No. I felt rather sorry for her.'

'What did she get up to while here?'

'She kept herself occupied and sat for ages making baby clothes. She went for regular walks and on Sundays she went to the local Baptist church but didn't make friends as she was quiet and reserved. We often went on tram rides into town together and she was very cheerful, so she wasn't trying to conceal herself in any way. She always wore black though.'

'And then what happened when the baby was born?' prompted Edwin.

At this point both sisters became very emotional and had trouble wiping away the tears.

'It was like this. Ted was true to his word and with the birth imminent, he acquired the services of a local doctor and a nurse named Mrs Wells to give her personal care. Phoebe and Ted were both excited about the birth and couldn't wait to see their child born. It was a pleasure to witness their joy. Then on Tuesday 18 July Phoebe suddenly suffered an awful fit entirely out of the blue. It was horrid to see and she fell unconscious. Well both of us were in a right state I can tell you. My sister went off to fetch the doctor while I sat with her. When the doctor arrived she was still unconscious on the floor and he examined her. She came round a bit but was delirious and weak and he believed she might have some form of anaemia or eclampsia. Then the nurse arrived and we managed to get her upstairs to her bed. Her condition was so bad that the life of the baby as well as the mother was at risk so he decided a caesarean operation was required. He left at went to Maidstone hospital to speak to a surgeon who offered to attend next day to perform the operation. Nurse Wells was wonderful and sat by her bedside all night.

The surgeon arrived with his equipment early next morning and a baby boy was born but was rather frail. Phoebe's condition was also worrying the doctors as the anaesthetic and operation had made her feebler and they discussed removing her to the hospital but decided to let her rest.

'Where was Ted all this time?'

'Well here's the thing. We were frantic because we had no contact address for him and of course Phoebe was unable to tell us as she couldn't speak clearly. He did not know any of this was happening. By chance Ted arrived early that afternoon for a visit oblivious to what had been happening. He rushed upstairs to Pheobe's bedside.

*

Edwin then interviewed Nurse Wells.

'I realise this may be upsetting but could you tell us what happened the afternoon of Phoebe's death?'

'After the baby was delivered I stayed with Miss Penniall all night and the next day caring for her and the baby as she was unable to. The father arrived early afternoon and was unaware of the situation. I heard a lot of shouting downstairs and a man crying out and then heard him running up the stairs. He sat on the bed sobbing, took her hand in his and was talking to her but of course getting no response said, "Oh Phoebe, don't you know me?' over and over again. He was in a terrible state weeping bitterly. He was inconsolable and went back downstairs in a state of panic. I stayed with her, but minutes later at about four o'clock she stretched out her hand and grabbed mine and seemed to struggle to say something, but I couldn't understand what she was saying. I knew she was dying at that point and went down to inform the father. He rushed out in a crazed state to fetch the doctor but by the time they returned she was dead.'

'How did Ted react to her death?'

'He was mortified and was overcome with grief and for the next few days hardly in contact with reality. He doted over his new born son cradling him for long periods and rocking him backward and forwards. He was then frantically rushing all over the place arranging things but did not seem in control of himself or what to do next.'

*

No sooner had the two doctors certified Phoebe's death as natural causes he registered her death under the name Phoebe Stanley and began organising her funeral. He also registered his son's birth under the name Edwin Alfred Stanley but for some reason this time used Pheobe's real surname as the mother on the death certificate. The sisters couldn't understand why he was in a such a hurry to have her buried. The hastily arranged funeral took place three days later on Saturday 22 July without informing her family or anyone else; He was in such turmoil that he was unable to understand the implications of what he was doing.

It was a no expense spared funeral with a closed hearse and a heavy polished oak coffin with silver plated mountings bearing the inscription "Phoebe Stanley died 19 July 1905 age 37." The hearse was followed by a solitary mourning coach containing Ted and the two Richardson sisters who were the only mourners. Her body was laid to rest in Maidstone cemetery with three beautiful wreaths placed on the grave but there was no headstone just the number forty on a wooden cross. That evening Ted returned in the carriage to the Richardson's and then paid a visit to the doctor to thank him and discuss the care of his son Edwin. The baby was very weak and frail and the doctor informed the saddened Ted that he didn't expect him to survive.

Ted told him that the two sisters had agreed to look after Edwin with the help of Mrs Wells and he would pay for all expenses incurred by them all. Two weeks after her death he collected his wife's belongings and visited his son whenever he could, unable to decide what to do with him. The sisters became very fond of him, saying he was a "delicate little fellow, the very image of his mother."

Then more tragedy struck when on August 11 Edwin sadly died causing great anguish to the sisters who had valiantly tried to keep him healthy but watched helplessly as he gradually deteriorated and slipped away. Ted was beside himself and found himself registering a second death within weeks. Meanwhile the Penniall family were oblivious to all these events and distraught about their missing daughter wondering what had happened to her.

*

Following further inquiries with the undertaker, the registrar and the bank used to pay all the expenses Edwin finally had the name of Phoebe's secret lover. His name was Edwin Alfred Stanton, a partner with his brother Horace in a Lewisham gold and silver wire company producing lace for officers uniforms based at the Armoury Mill. He was a tall gentlemanly looking man of dark complexion with a slight build and a pencil ginger moustache. He lived with his wife Rosetta in a large house on Dartmouth Row hung with creepers and shaded by trees on the edge of Greenwich Park: as far away from the poverty and life of Phoebe as you could get. His wife was fourteen years his senior which may have influenced his decision to enter into an affair with a younger woman. He was a chapel goer often addressing religious meetings and a supporter of mission work in Deptford and Greenwich. His home was very close to where Phoebe was living which had been a bonus for the couple when they were courting.

The mystery of Phoebe's disappearance had for months been covered extensively and dramatically by the London Press and local newspapers. It was a true mystery story that captivated readers, helped by sensational headlines such as the *Daily Mirror* headline on the 25 August, "Is she Married, or Dead and Buried, or in Hiding." When the news finally broke in the newspapers on the 29 August 1905 that he was the father of the child and the centre of police investigations it proved a sensation and his house was soon besieged. The previous day he had finally confessed to Rosetta and left the house in a distressed state, but did not go to work and disappeared leaving her worried about his safety. The *Daily Mirror* managed to gain an interview with the equally distressed Rosetta and reported:

> Full of dread, Mrs Stanton then unfolded the papers and read the latest news of the tragedy which had brought so much sorrow to her home. She read how Mr Stanton, a chapel goer, who had the respect of all who knew him, was accused of being the father of a child, the birth of which at Maidstone cost Phoebe Penniall her life. "I know nothing but what I have seen in the newspapers," said the distressed Mrs Stanton to a *Daily Mirror* reporter yesterday. "I am too much upset to think of anything else, but although I keep on thinking I cannot explain. It has been an awful blow. There must be some explanation. He is as much distressed as I am. He went out this morning quite broken hearted and I was afraid he might do something unmentionable."

The newspaper went on to add that:

> Mr Stanton is expecting a summons for having registered the child's birth and the woman's death under the false name of Stanley instead of Penniall. This being the case, he refuses to make a statement. Mrs Stanton added, 'If one is issued it will be in the form of a message, but of course, he may take no notice of the attacks made-up on him.'

He did find support amongst some of his close friends. "I believe him to be an honourable man, who will turn a deaf ear to the voices of slander,' said a prominent non-conformist who knows Mr Stanton personally. 'After all, he was only done his duty in trying to shield the woman. Refusing to explain circumstances which are compromising is quixotic, but it is just like old Stanton.

Many other people in Blackheath and Lewisham though were less sympathetic, shrugging their shoulders and saying 'You never really know. We have often heard of Stanton addressing religious meetings. But there you go.'

The Yard interviewed Edwin Stanton and were unable to shed more light on his deplorable behaviour in lying and not communicating with her parents of her whereabouts or even her death, and his cruel action of burying her without inviting them. The family had been caused unimaginable hurt and distress without reason but he had not committed any crime. Edwin considered prosecuting for having registered the child's birth and the woman's death under a false name, but having interviewed the two doctors was satisfied there was no grounds for suspecting foul play in connection with her disappearance so the matter was not pursued. Nor was there any case of bigamy as he never legally married her.

A last word from one local newspaper summing up the story for its readers was less than sympathetic: "The whole story which was told with such sensational embellishments in some London newspapers thus proves to be nothing more or less than an everyday tale of a woman's love and downfall."

*

Edwin and Tom were standing in one of the "best parts" of Maidstone cemetery staring down at the rather forlorn graves of Phoebe Penniall and her son Edwin.

'I think this is one the strangest cases I have investigated,' stated Edwin.

'I agree with you there, Sarge. Me too,' agreed Tom.

'The tragedy is that in our modern world all this should have been unnecessary.'

'How's that?'

'She could have been at home with the support of her parents and family possibly having the baby without any problem, but instead through fear of being ostracised and having her reputation tarnished she had, like a common criminal, been forced to go on the run so to speak.'

'I see what you mean.'

'Society and its outdated taboos has a lot to answer for,' sighed Edwin and they turned and silently walked out the cemetery. Edwin was commended for his diligence in tracing her despite all the efforts to throw everyone off the scent.

9

Rope and Ladder Robbery at Vitners (1900)

One of the few lucky bobbies with any form of transport.

On the afternoon of Thursday 15 November a train pulled into Maidstone East station from London Victoria. Amongst the throng of passengers that alighted were four individual men all dressed like workmen and each carrying a bulky canvas haversack over their shoulder. They kept separated so as not to draw attention to themselves and exited the station and headed up to Mote Park to a prearranged spot where they met up. They greeted each other and sat down for a smoke discussing their plan so that each one fully understood his role. One of them had come down from London a week earlier to "case" and make a rough plan of the house and garden. He noted where the dogs were kept, how many staff there were and the evening routine. They were feeling confident and as dusk fell they headed into the vast Vinter estate. At its centre was a mansion owned by the Whatman family since 1782, having been passed down the generations until the eldest son James Whatman IV inherited it in 1852. He made extensive alterations adding many rooms and constructing many outbuildings to make it a true country estate. These included a dairy, brew house, larder, servants hall, pantry, study and bathroom. Outside a walled kitchen garden, icehouse, boat house and landscaped grounds with many exotic trees and plants, and extensive stables were also added.

The family were the most important paper makers in Britain with a mill just south of the estate. Their paper was of high quality and in great demand and they invented woven and antiquarian paper highly popular with printers and artists. James twice became the local MP for Maidstone and having no sons the house and estate was left on his death in 1887 to his daughters. In November 1900 his widow Mrs Whatman was still living in the house along with her youngest daughter Louisa and an extensive staff, but this did not worry the four men now prowling the estate. The house was crammed with over a century of family heirlooms and ripe for pillaging. The house burnt down in 1950 coinciding with the death of the last remaining daughter, and it was demolished in 1952 and the estate sold off.

The four men were by no mere amateurs but a professional gang of burglars. As dusk fell they quite brazenly walked up a track heading for the house without being challenged, but they were short of a specific piece of equipment: a ladder. This was remedied when they passed an orchard belonging to a Mr. Lockyer and spotted a discarded ladder with a few rungs missing. Being in no hurry and good at improvising they stopped and mended it with a wooden stake from a nearby hedgerow. Deciding it was too long to carry, they used a knife to shorten it before stealing it and carrying on walking.

The damp and cold was beginning to chill them as they crouched surveying the house from a distance. It was their bold plan to rob the house while the owners were eating dinner and the staff busy serving them which was a time-honoured strategy of professional burglars when raiding palatial homes which due to their size are viewed as particularly vulnerable. They intended to use what was called in the trade the "Rope and Ladder Robbery;" a well-known and elaborate method when entrance to the house is made through a bedroom window by ladder and all entrances and exits are barred by securing the doors with ropes. As a further precaution against surprise by the police they would use another well-known trick of the trade by placing ropes across pathways leading to the property to trip up or hamper anyone who might chase them while they made their escape.

On reaching the grand house they started work in earnest. They silenced the watch dogs with the drugged meat they had brought with them and began unravelling coils of rope from their sacks and proceeded to lay the trip ropes at ankle level across the exterior doors and some of the pathways leading to the house. If they were discovered and had to make a run for it they hoped anyone giving chase would come a cropper giving them time to escape. Having completed this task they put the ladder up to a bedroom window. They believed they had timed it well to coincide with dinner time and the staff would be busy in the kitchen and serving table, but what they had not accounted for was Louisa Whatman, the youngest daughter, deciding to let the indoor pet dogs out of the courtyard door at 8pm for a toilet break before dinner. As she tried to open the door it caught on the rope, but it was so slack that she was able to force it a few inches and peering round the door she spotted the rope and immediately knew what was happening. She was aware of this method as it was a talking point at many society dinners.

Frenzied activity then occurred as she ran down the corridor shouting for the footman, telling him to force his way out of the back door if necessary and raise the alarm with the police. He rushed to the stables and without saddling one of the horses jumped on it and galloped bareback down the driveway towards town and Wrens Cross police station, just a mile and a half away. Just prior to this uproar the rather tardy old Mrs Whatman was still in her bedroom getting ready for dinner when she heard scraping at her bedroom window and looking round spotted the ghostly face of someone outside. One of the men was at the top of the ladder with a jemmy trying to open it. She screamed for her maid which resulted in the man sliding in shock down the ladder and running off in the wake of his three comrades. The game seemed up.

The footman had reached the police station, jumped off the horse, and ran into the front office bumping into Edwin and Superintendent Lane, the deputy Chief Constable who were discussing a matter there. Having calmed the excited footman and heard his story they shouted for every available officer to follow them to Vinters. They arrived within half an hour and Edwin placed a cordon of constables at intervals to search the grounds while he and the superintendent searched the house but they were too late - the men had long gone. Edwin and his men then searched in the town for any suspicious looking characters to no avail but next morning a witness at the railway station told them he had seen two rough looking men catch the 7.23am London Chatham and Dover train to London. Edwin immediately telegraphed Scotland Yard who met the train at Victoria station but they found no men of the description exiting the train. Whoever they were it was apparent they must have alighted at another station en route and escaped.

10

A Servant's Terrible Plight (1912)

At the end of March 1912, Ada Jeffery, a 25-year-old single woman arrived at Combe Bank, a grand palladian style house situated on a huge estate near the village of Sundridge, just outside Sevenoaks in Kent. She was there for an interview and walked round to the rear kitchen entrance gazing in awe at the fine gardens and statues. She was not overawed having worked as a house servant before but never in such a large busy household and had in fact just returned from a job in Ireland.

The mansion was owned by Mr Robert Ludwig Mond, the son of Ludwig Mond a leading chemist and industrialist, the co-owner of Brunner, Mond & Co one of the four major chemical companies which became ICI in 1926. Robert inherited the Company and Combe Bank on the death of his father in 1907. The house was vast with a ballroom, theatre, stables, walled kitchen garden and dozens of rooms. Robert built a laboratory in the stables to continue his experiments and was a very rich man having discovered a gaseous compound called nickel carbonyl. He also had a great interest in archaeology and had worked with the likes of Howard

Carter in Egypt, so the house was full of artefacts. He was a generous benefactor to many causes particularly those involving children. His wife had died in 1905, and he lived alone with a legion of servants and workers. His housekeeper was desperate to replace a kitchen maid who had recently left.

Ada was determined to get the job and make an immediate good impression. The urgency revolved round her recent weight gain which she had made a good attempt at hiding with baggy clothes. Taking a deep intake of breath she knocked on the door and was taken into the large kitchen by the housekeeper, Mrs Blisset who sat her down by the huge fireplace and read her references. The interview went well as Mrs Blisset wasn't too bothered who she took on as she was leaving the employment herself in a week's time and knew that if Ada wasn't up to scratch it wouldn't be her problem. She gave Ada the job and a few days later on the 31 March she returned with her belongings in her trunk and was taken right up to the top floor to the servants quarters where she was shown her room and introduced to her roommate scullery maid Elsie Fraser.

Ada awoke next morning after a sleepless night when she heard Elsie dressing. It was 5.30am and Elsie had to be in the kitchen by 6am to get the range hot enough to boil water for the tea and then wash up any breakfast utensils. Ada as a kitchen maid usually received an extra hour before descending to start preparing breakfast. She got on relatively well with Elsie and as the days past she made every attempt to disguise her condition from her. Elsie though soon became suspicious but never mentioned it.

Robert Mond had a private secretary named Mr Matthew Cowap and he was a very busy man flitting about the house giving commands and explaining what was required of the staff. Being such a prominent and rich businessman, his employer often travelled to London for meetings when not working from home. The house was always busy particularly at weekends when he entertained house guests which put great demands on the staff. Mr Cowap visited the kitchen most days to speak to Annie Woodward the cook to inform her of what was required, and he had noticed Ada on these visits and observed that she seemed pale and sickly. He relied on the housekeeper to take on staff and rarely intervened in her decisions, but he was distinctly worried about the new girl and kept a close watch on her viewing her as a slacker. On several occasions he considered sacking her as there was something not just right with her. As the weeks passed he noticed she seemed to be more lethargic and gaining weight. By the fifth week of her service he was definitely suspicious of her condition and wished he had dismissed her when he first thought there was a problem.

On Saturday morning the 4 May he decided it was time to have a word about the matter with Mrs Woodward and he went to the kitchen but only found Ada there. He inquired the whereabouts of the cook and she informed him that she was upstairs attending to a matter which made it awkward as he needed her present when he spoke to Ada. He told her he would come back to see her when the cook returned which obviously worried her. But he was tied up all day with Mr Mond in his laboratory and didn't have time to return.

That evening Elsie and Ada retired to bed at 10.15pm, thoroughly worn out after a busy day as Mr Mond had several house guests. Elsie fell asleep straight away, but Ada was not feeling too well with stomach pains and tossed and turned until about 4am when she couldn't stand the pain any longer and got up. She went to Elsie's bed and shook her awake. She woke in a daze to find her roommate standing over her which made her start.

'Whatever's wrong Ada?' moaned Elsie, 'have I overslept?'

'No. I'm not feeling well Elsie.'

'What's wrong with you?' she inquired getting up and lighting a lamp.

'I've got terrible pain in my stomach and feel very weak, and I need something hot to drink,' said Ada laying back on her bed.

Elsie looked down at her and watched her holding her stomach, 'You do look terrible pale I must say. I'll get some water with a drop of brandy from the kitchen.'

She came back five minutes later and offered it to Ada who put it to her lips and then felt nauseous, so she put the glass down.

'Try and sleep. I'm sure you'll feel better in the morning.'

Ada laid in bed becoming quite distressed and unable to sleep because the pain was worsening. After a quarter of an hour she called out to Elsie again and woke her. 'I've got a horrid taste in my mouth can you get me a cup of tea?'

'You'd better drink it this time. I've got to be at work soon.' Elsie got up again lit the lamp and went downstairs to make her a cup of tea. On her return Ada could not swallow it, and Elsie was getting annoyed.

They both laid in bed, Ada writhing in pain and moaning while Elsie listened. At 5.30am Elsie got up and got dressed to go down to work. Ada asked for yet another cup of tea and told her to tell the cook she couldn't come down.

'Cook ain't going to be pleased.'

Elsie explained to Annie the cook what had transpired during the night and that she was worried about her roommate believing there was more to it than just stomach pains. She gave a big sigh, washed her hands and dried them on her apron and said to Elsie, 'right then, let's go and see what's ailing her. We'll all be getting into trouble thanks to that girl if the work doesn't get done.' She stomped up the several flights of stairs, went into the bedroom and sat on the bed, putting her hand to Ada's forehead to check her temperature and asked her about her symptoms. She told her to rest and went back down to the kitchen returning later with a light breakfast of toast which again Ada was unable to eat. Feeling sick she stumbled to the bathroom and sat by the toilet. Annie left her there as she had to prepare breakfast for the household.

Annie later sent the housemaid Jean Ritchie to find out how Ada was faring.

'I am still in terrible pain.'

'Do you think you have a chill. Do you want a hot water bottle?' asked Jean.

'I've already got one, but it is not helping.'

Jean went back downstairs but after an hour Annie told Jean to go back up to check again but when she got there at 10.30am the door was locked, and she couldn't get in. She knocked several times but there was no reply, so she went back downstairs to tell Annie who on hearing that the door was locked became alarmed and hurried back upstairs, knocked and shouted through the door.

'Who's there?' called Ada.

'It's only me, cook. Let me in.'

'Give me a minute or two.'

'What's going on in there, let me in we're worried about you.'

Annie could hear her moving about and after five minutes she unlocked the door.

'Whatever is the matter with you?' she asked. 'I can't leave you like this. I'm going to see the master and get him to call a doctor.'

'Please cook, don't do that. I am feeling better now.'

'I'm not putting up with any more of your nonsense.'

Annie guessed that Ada was in trouble and desperately needed help and Mr Mond gave permission for Dr Stanley E Ward of Brasted, the family doctor, to be called, and he arrived at 11am and

Jean took him to Ada's room. She informed him of the stomach pains that had plagued her throughout the night and he examined her and soon realised what the ailment was as she was haemorrhaging. As luck would have it one of the house guests that weekend was the well-known Dr. Ralph Vincent, of 1 Harley Street, an obstetric specialist. He was a great friend of Robert Mond and a regular visitor. In 1904 Ralph had established an infant's hospital in Hampstead which soon became overwhelmed, so Robert stepped in and built and equipped a purpose-built hospital in Vincent Square, Victoria, London in memory of his late wife. It was opened by the Duchess of Albany in 1907 and had wards for fifty children.

Dr. Ward went down to the drawing room and explained what was happening and Ralph agreed to examine Ada. He immediately realised that she had very recently given birth but seemed oblivious to what had happened which was worrying. The two men left the room without commenting to her, not wishing to distress her further. They decided to let her calm down and rest before trying to establish what she had done with the baby.

After discussing the matter with Robert Mond, it was decided to send Jean Ritchie to Ada to try and discover the whereabouts of the baby. Jean had been working there for a year and was at the time the responsible servant in the absence of any housekeeper and helped Ada settle in. Their paths only crossed occasionally during work and so Jean had not got to know her that well, but Mr Mond thought it best. So Jean had the unenviable task of talking to Ada who continually sobbed but finally Jean coaxed her into admitting she'd had a child while in the bathroom earlier that day and had smothered its cries by stuffing a gag in its mouth. She had then locked it in her tin box where she kept all her belongings.

Jean asked Ada for the keys to the box which she gave her indicating which key opened it. Jean asked her if it was born alive and she said yes and then bravely and tentatively unlocked the box and discovered the child's body covered up and obviously not moving. Jean rushed back downstairs to report back to the doctors that she had found the body. They returned to the room where Ada was in a state of extreme distress so they sedated her and retrieved the body taking it downstairs to a back room where they examined it. The baby was wrapped in a piece of striped skirting and a jacket which completely enveloped the head and was tied round the neck. On untying the cloth the doctors found the mouth to be filled with a long piece of rag which had been pushed in with such force it had extended the jaws so much as to tear the mouth into the cheek. It was a gruesome spectacle. Throughout the whole episode Ada was described as being completely detached and not seeming "to realise quite what had happened."

They then went down to see Mond to explain the terrible situation.

'The police must be informed as soon as possible,' said Dr. Ward.

'Of course, Of course, I will get onto it straight away,' replied a rather disconcerted Mond.

'Ada seems to have lapsed into some kind of shocked state, and I am not happy she should be left alone for her own safety,' directed Dr Ward.

'Do you think she might, you know, harm herself or worse,' tentatively asked Mond who was himself rather shocked.

'Quite possible in these circumstances.'

'My God,' exclaimed Mond.

'I would suggest a nurse should be with her at all times until the police decide what to do.'

'I will get Elsie her roommate to keep an eye on her.'

'Excellent.'

'We have sedated her so she should sleep for a while.'

*

Edwin received the news of the possible infanticide at 9pm that evening and Mond sent his car and driver to collect him. Dr Ward had gone home, but he was met by Dr. Vincent who showed him the body. Edwin had seen such awful sights many times before, but he still hated to see these poor mites particularly when they had suffered injuries and distress. He asked Mond that rather than leaving the body in the house, was there anywhere else on the estate that it could be moved to. He said there was an empty cottage, so Edwin reverently removed the body there. As Ada was sleeping under sedation he saw no reason to disturb her that night so returned to Sevenoaks police station. He reported the case personally next morning to the Coroner in Tunbridge Wells and the two men travelled to the estate. Dr Ward gave Edwin the rag from the baby's mouth and the clothing that the baby was found wrapped in.

Ada was not in a fit state to be interviewed until Wednesday but in the meantime Edwin searched the room she was in and her belongings and found new baby clothes in her trunk which surprised him. Edwin cautioned her, 'You will have to be taken into custody on a charge of suspicion of wilfully causing the death of your child on the 5 May 1912 at Coombe Bank, Sundridge.

Dr Batchelor Taylor in Sevenoaks completed a post mortem next morning and confirmed the body was of a fully developed male child with no injuries except to the mouth. The lungs floated in water and other evidence showed that in his opinion the child had been born alive. Death was by asphyxia from suffocation and he sadly noted that the rag had been forcibly pushed into the mouth and prevented from falling out by tying the jacket round the neck.

*

The inquest was held in the Garden Cottage at Coombe Bank on Wednesday 8 May before divisional Coroner Thomas Buss and after preliminary evidence was adjourned for two weeks until 22 May to allow the police to gather more evidence. Ada was present at the next inquest having recovered somewhat but she still n an emotional state, constantly sobbing as the evidence was against her was given.

The main discussion was on whether the baby was born alive as if this was the case Ada would be facing a murder charge, if not she would receive a lesser charge when appearing at the Magistrates hearing. Jean Rirchie was asked:

'I suppose at the time you spoke to Ada Jeffrey she was very bad?'

'She seemed in severe pain.'

'Are you quite sure she understood your question in the bedroom when you asked her about the child being born alive?'

'Oh yes. I think so?'

This was obviously very damning for Ada, but the hearing soon turned into a battle between the doctors over the issue, and it was very lucky for Ada that the eminent Dr Vincent had been visiting that weekend.

Ada's defence lawyer Mr H F Colam was quick to cast doubt on the testimony of the two local doctors who were both convinced that the baby was born alive and had breathed.

'Why is that doctor?'

'We conducted tests on the lungs and there was evidence of air having been in the lungs.'

Mr Colom said, ' Is that conclusive?

Doctor Ward answered, 'Yes, I think so.'

Mr Colam then asked: 'So you say you think it was conclusive but nevertheless I understand you then tested in another way using a small piece of heart in order to exclude the possibility of error. Is that so?'

'Yes.'

'Was that test conclusive?'

'Yes.'

'So why not make the test on the heart in the first instance if that is conclusive and the other one isn't?'

'It is the usual custom to do it that way.'

'I put it to you as a well-known doctor that neither of these tests is conclusive. It is the best you can do, but it is not conclusive. Is that right doctor?'

Ward answered, 'I, as a doctor, would consider it was conclusive. But in my experience in making post mortems of infants it was not sufficient to enable me to give a definite opinion.'

The defence lawyer then queried Doctor Batchelor Taylor's conclusions.

'You agree with the evidence presented by Dr. Ward?'

'I heard the evidence of Doctor Ward as to the post mortem examination which I assisted him to make and I agree with that evidence. The test applied was not absolutely positive, but I would say the balance of evidence was in favour of the child having breathed. There was no sign of blueness on the neck.'

Colam then called Doctor Ralph Vincent who stated he had been senior resident medical officer of Queen Charlotte's Lying In Hospitals and was presently senior physician to the Infant Hospital in London.

The defence lawyer asked him, 'you attended the child, did you not?'

'I did.'

'And when you examined the child it had a wad in its mouth?'

'It did.'

'Are you satisfied that the child ever breathed at all?'

'I am not.'

'Can you tell us why you say that?'

'I came to this conclusion from the extreme pallor of the child and the absence of any indication that it had breathed making it quite inconsistent in my opinion with the theory that the child had died from suffocation.'

'Was the rag put in the mouth with the intent to kill or only to stop the cries.'

'Stopping the cries of a newly born infant would amount to pretty much the same thing.'

Mr Colam then addressed the jury at length and said they had heard from Superintendent Edwin Fowle that there was a suggestion that the charge against the girl will be that of murder. Of course the jurymen would take their law from the Coroner, who would direct them as to what they should take into consideration when they came to discuss their verdict, but he did suggest that if they were asked to find a verdict in consonance with what suggestion made by the Superintendent they should hesitate very long before doing so. After referring to the state of mind in which the mother found herself, he went on to say that they knew the child was born and that it was not of premature birth, but before the jury could even think of a charge of murder, they had to be satisfied that there was an independent human being in existence who could be killed, because it was not murder unless an independent human existence was there to be destroyed.

After hearing an eloquent appeal on behalf of the mother of the child by Mr: Colam, the Coroner reviewed the evidence and told the jury that he must ask them to give answers to the following questions. One, has it been proved to your satisfaction that the child, the subject of this inquiry, was the child of Ada Jeffrey? Two, has it also been proved to your satisfaction that the child was born alive? Three, was it also proved that the child sustained violence or actually came by its death by violence? Four, and in that case, does the evidence lead you to connect any person with having committed that violence towards the deceased child?

The jury then retired to another room to consider their verdict. And after an absence of an hour and a quarter, they returned and the foreman stood and informed the court that they had concluded that the child was still born. The coroner then thanked the jury for the time and trouble they had given to the case. The foreman then said, 'are we now exempt for the next ten years? And the coroner replied, 'I hope you will be, but I cannot promise.'

Ada appeared before the Magistrates at the Sevenoaks Police Court before Mr W Crosby Hill, the chairman and Mr P Batticombe charged with on the 5th of May in the Parish of Sundridge, being then delivered of a certain male child, and unlawfully, by a certain secret disposition of the dead body of the child, did endeavour to conceal the birth there contrary to the Statute. As the Inquest had determined that the baby was stillborn the murder charge had been dropped to concealment of birth, which at the time was a frequently used as courts became more enlightened to the social and mental health aspects surrounding women giving birth.

Dr. Vincent reiterated that the appearance of the child was inconsistent with suffocation, and he was satisfied that the child had breathed. He did not think that the tests made by Dr. Ward were quite conclusive and that he could not say that the wad was forced into the mouth or not. Ada was committed to the next Maidstone Assizes under the charge of attempting to conceal the body.

The Maidstone Assizes were held on Tuesday 25 June and presided over by Lord Chief Justice Alverstone. Mr Thesiger defended Ada and Mr Dickens prosecuted. Ada was once again distraught and had to be consoled, but she was charged with the lesser crime of concealing the birth of her child at Sundridge and pleaded guilty. Thanks to Dr. Vincent she had avoided a charge of murder.

In an act of immense compassion Robert Mond made the court aware that he wished Ada to continue in his service on a temporary basis if the Court could see its way to discharge her. Receiving no complaint from the prosecution the Judge bound Ada over in her own recognisance and she was released into Robert Mond's care. She could not have dreamed of a better outcome to her predicament. If Ada had been working in most other households this would never been the outcome, but she was lucky in finding the support of Robert Mond and Ralph Vincent.

11

The Life and Career of Edwin Fowle 1872 – 1944

Edwin Fowle, badge number 287, was a much-esteemed decorated Kent County Constabulary police officer with many accolades including a police merit star and over twenty commendations and was a pioneer of modern investigative policing in Kent and yet his contribution to the force has been forgotten by history and the force itself.

He had a long and illustrious career completing an exemplary and extraordinary 42 years of loyal service from a constable in October 1890 to superintendent in charge of his own division in 1911 and retirement in 1932.

Edwin was born into a police family dynasty in 1872 in the small village of Preston situated between Canterbury and Ramsgate in the County of Kent, England; his father was a superintendent, his elder brother Thomas also rose to the rank of superintendent, his younger brother Ivo to Inspector and one of his uncles was a railway detective. In his first six years he was

Detective Inspector Edwin Fowle (1908)

Courtesy Alamy Images

posted to Gillingham, Westgate, Dartford, Ightham and Malling learning on the job and from "old hands" as there was no set training. He gained considerable experience, catching the eye of his superiors who immediately acknowledged him as a rising star with an aptitude for investigative work.

In 1896 he was a founding member of the Constabulary's Detective Department at their Wrens Court, Maidstone Headquarters when he became one of their first detective constables. In 1900 he was promoted to First Class Detective Sergeant and became head of the department and in 1906 become the first Detective Inspector in the history of the Kent force. This small unit of a sergeant and three constables was the equivalent of the modern Flying Squad established to investigate serious crime across the whole 1,368 square miles of the County of mostly rural countryside and scattered population.

His time as a detective spanned exactly the Edwardian era and his beat was the entire County of Kent investigating a wide range of crimes including murder, infanticide, child rape, robbery, burglary, fraud, arson, pickpocketing, vagrancy, alcoholism and drug addiction. He was highly regarded and recognised throughout the County of Kent particularly amongst pickpockets who he took a special interest in. In his early days as a detective, he knew all the leading notorious London and Kent pickpocket gangs and they knew him to their cost, but the criminal fraternity had a guarded respect for him and referred to him as "The Pickpocket Terror."

He made quite a name for himself as a detective becoming one of the most recognised officers across the County and although he made every effort to shun the press and publicity and never gave interviews he was ever in the newspapers due to the many headline cases he investigated.

He was not of a striking appearance being only five feet nine inches tall, but he was broad shouldered and of stout stature with a well-groomed large moustache below a substantial nose. He was always smartly dressed and always wearing the fashionable derby hat. His main attribute was a questioning mind and a tenacious nature, perfect qualities for a detective. He was described as a driven and religious man with a great sense of duty and a stickler for correct police procedure and record keeping which his superiors and the judiciary were complimentary about.

He got married on the 9th. November 1910 in St Michaels Church, Beckenham to Annie Sophia Vockins. Edwin remained with the detective department until his promotion on the 20th. April 1911 to the rank of Superintendent when he became head of the Sevenoaks Division. While at Sevenoaks he was very popular with his men, the public, counsel, solicitors, magistrates and local authorities. He was known for encouraging his men in their recreations especially his favourite sports cricket and rifle shooting and tutored and encouraged them in first aid. He orchestrated the rescue of over seventy injured and dead passengers involved in the disastrous 1927 Sevenoaks train crash which killed twelve people during which his men put their first aid skills to good use.

In total his career spanned the reigns of four monarchs, and he experienced the emergence of motor vehicles, extensive train lines, telephones, radio, major advances in forensic science and innovations in policing methods as well as social transformations and changes in criminal behaviour which he seems to have taken all in his stride managing to adapt to all the new challenges.

He was to investigate many murders in the eleven years from 1900-1910 as a detective across the whole County of Kent and still more on his promotion back to uniform. Much to his undoubted satisfaction and the gratitude of the County he managed to solve most of them but there were some he failed on. A case in point was his most sensational and renowned case - the 1908 Seal Chart murder of Caroline Luard wife of Major-General Charles Luard. It was a murder and story straight from the annals of Agatha Christie. A society wife shot dead in the head in a summerhouse by an unknown assailant and an assortment intrigue.

His first headline murder case which resulted in nationwide sensational coverage occurred just months after his promotion to Detective Sergeant and head of the Kent Detective Department. On a bleak New Year's Eve 1901, a 7-year-old girl was abducted, outraged and murdered and her body cruelly discarded in the icy waters of the village pond in the serene village of Southborough near Tonbridge in Kent The crime sent shockwaves through all echelons of Edwardian Society and the town soon descended into chaos, besieged by the national press and hordes of morbid sightseers, Edwin Fowle and his detectives had to sift through a web of conflicting witness accounts to finally track down a prime suspect but a possible accomplice writing menacing letters complicated the case. The full story from the point of view of all those involved is recreated in a gripping narrative by the author in his book "The Tonbridge Outrage."

Another of his headline cases involved a man brutally attacked at midnight in a church meadow in a small hamlet near Tenterden in 1905 with his throat gruesomely cut from ear to ear and his skull bludgeoned. The body laid undiscovered for thirty hours and once found caused disbelief and shock in the community and once again garnered national press coverage. A band of newly arrived Algerian hawkers roaming the area intensified the drama. Edwin helped by a cast of villagers as witnesses, manged to piece together the events leading up to the event. His investigation earned him a commendation and a police medal. The full story can be found in The Tenterden Murder by the author.

He retired in December 1932 and remained in Sevenoaks. His obituary described him as having a great sense of duty, a driven man, who was religious and inspired by God to maintain peace in the world. He died peacefully aged 74 in Holmesdale Hospital Sevenoaks in 1944.

12

Selected References

Kent Archives, Maidstone

Records of Service (1857-1899) C/PO/22/5/1; 22/5/2; 22/5/3; 22/5/4, 22/5/5.

Inherited Local Force General Personnel Records (1869-1922)

The Kent Police Centenary – Recollections of a Hundred Years, Centenary Booklet Sub-Committee, Edited R.L.Thomas, 1957.

Bad or Mad? Infanticide: Insanity and Morality in Nineteenth Century Britain

https://www.midlandshistoricalreview.com/20200513_bador-mad/

Infanticide : its law, prevalence, prevention and history / by William Burke Ryan. Public Domain Mark. Source: Wellcome Collection. https://wellcomecollection.org/works/q579d2ft

T. H. Rose, The People's Important Guide (1847)

M. Jackson (ed.), *Infanticide: Historical Perspectives on Child Murder and Concealment, 1550-2000* (Aldershot, 2002) 'The Execution of Mrs Winsor' (1865),

Mrs Baines, Journal of Social Sciences 1866 (Infanticide)

Chapter 1

The Courier 4 April 1907, Six Weeks for a Welsher, p11.

Herne Bay Press, 22 June 1907, From All Quarters, p6.

Maidstone and Kentish Journal 16 April 1908, Notes and Comments.

The Courier, 12 April 1907, George Pearce Welsher.

Folkestone Express, 1 December 1900, The Welsher at the Folkestone races, p8.

Kent Gazette, 11 April 1908, Saffer case.

John Bull, 6 June 1908, Racing Notes.

Chapter 2

Bromley Telegraph & Chislehurst Chronicle, 29 December 1906, Murder Charge at Bromley, An Infants tragic Death.

St Pancras Chronicle, 4 January 1907, A St Pancras Waif. p6.

The Bromley Telegraph & Chislehurst Chronicle 5 January 1907, The Knockholt Murder Charge, p8.

Tonbridge Free Press, 1 March 1907, County News, p2.

Bromley & West Kent Telegraph, 2 March 1907, Kent Winter Assizes, Local Cases, p3.

Chapter 3

The Free Press 1 March 1902, The Tonbridge Romance, Field Pleads Guilty, p3.

Maidstone Journal and Kentish Advertiser, 2 January 1902, Sterling Defence.

Kentish Express and Ashford News, 1 March 1902, Kent Assizes, p6.

Maidstone and Kentish Journal, 26 December 1901, A Tonbridge Lady Duped.

Maidstone & Kentish Journal, 2 Jan 1902, Romance prisoner Again Before Magistrates, p4.

Kent and Sussex Courier, 27 December 1901, The Romance at Tonbridge, A Lady Broken Down.

The Tonbridge Press, 28 December 1901, A Tonbridge Romance, A Young Lady and Her

Money.

The Sevenoaks Chronicle, 3 January 1902, Romantic Engagement and Sequel.

Kent & Sussex Courier, 1 January 1902, The Alleged Heartless Fraud of Tonbridge Lady, p2.

Old Bailey Procedures, Category Imprisonment, Sub category Hard labour def1-763-18840623-763 Offence theft, simple larceny, sexual offence, Bigamy. Joseph Field alias Rolf (b1862 age 23) Stealing sheets, pillow slips, blankets, other goods, of Clarissa Taylor 23/6/1884 with Rebecca Field nee Newman.

St Martins in The Field church record No 377 13 June 1901 Joseph Pope Field aged 38 was married to a Frances Taylor aged 56 widow. Father Thomas Field listed as a merchant was present and the bride's father William Parker, a retired army officer. Witnesses HE Jollee & R Bennett

Chapter 4

The Reporter, 21 September 1907, Meopham Sensation, p2.

Chapter 5

Folkestone Express, Sandgate & Hythe Advertiser. 2 December 1903. p7.

Folkestone Express, 29 July 1903, The Baby Murder at Hythe, p8.

Folkestone Herald, 25 July 1903, Alleged Child Murder, p12.

Folkestone Hythe, Sandgate Herald, 28 November 1903, Concealment of Birth, p6.

Folkestone Herald, 1 August 903, Alleged Child Murder, p10.

Folkestone Express, 2 December 1903, A Pathetic Scene. p7.

Hythe History blog, The Many Causes of Sarah Kingsley by Anne Petrie 9 June 2019.

Chapter 6

The Free Press, 31 January 1908, Bold Burglars, p5.

The Free Press 28 February 1908, The Hadlow Burglary, p2.

*Kentish Express,*1 February 1908, A Mansion Raided, p8.

The Free Press, 28 February1908, Kent Winter Assizes, p2.

The Courier, 31 Jan 1908, Burglary at Hadlow, p11.

Chapter 7

The Courier, 1 September 1905, Sevenoaks Mystery.

The Daily News, 26 August 1905, Mystery of Kentish Farm, p7.

*The Daily Mirror,*28 August 1905, Life Tragedy of Phoebe Penniall, p4.

Daily Mirror, 29 August 1905, Kentish Romance, Wife's Touching Faith. p5.

Illustrated Police News, 2 September 1905, A Painful Romance.

Salisbury Times & Gazette, 1 September 1905, Kentish Mystery Solved, p3.

Chapter 8

Maidstone & Kentish Journal, 22 November 1900, Attempted Burglary at Vintners, p8.

Sevenoaks Chronicle, 23 November 1900, Ingenious Burglars, p7.

Folkestone Express, 28 November 1900, Extraordinary Attempt at Burglary, p3.

Chapter 9

The Courier, 10 May 1912, A Child's Death, A Servant's Terrible Plight, p12.

Sevenoaks Chronicle & Kentish Advertiser, 24 May 1912, The Sundridge Tragedy.

Sevenoaks Chronicle, 10 May 1912, Distressing Affair at Sundridge, p8.

Kent & Sussex Courier, 10 May 1912, p5.

Discover The Edwardian Detective Edwin Fowle Series

The Tonbridge Outrage